AMERICA'S GOVERNMENTS

ENEMIES OF THE POOR

Praise for
America's Governments: Enemies of the Poor

Archie Richards' book is not only intelligent and erudite; it is heart-felt and authentic. It is the plea of a brilliant man who knows that there is no life, no society, no country, without freedom as a first principle.

– Jeffrey A. Tucker, AIER

I don't know Archie Richards, but I sure wish he lived next door if he is even half as delightfully informed and irreverent in person as he comes across in *America's Governments, Enemies of the Poor.* The book details 38 major ways that governments impoverish all Americans, with esoteric policies like the Davis-Bacon and Jones Acts and ubiquitous ones like lotteries and Social Security. By the end, readers will not want to defund the police; they will want to defund (most of) the government, especially the monstrosities in Washington, Albany, Boston, Sacramento, Springfield, and Trenton.

– Robert E. Wright, AIER

After a long career in finance and writing newspaper columns, Archie Richards has collected several years of his libertarian writings into a great book. While I agree with just about all of his views – his proposals regarding the great American game of baseball is one I respectfully, if vociferously, disagree with – I'm nevertheless extremely happy that they are compiled in a way that will see their wider diffusion.

– Pete Earle, AIER

AMERICA'S GOVERNMENTS

ENEMIES OF THE POOR

ARCHIE RICHARDS

DEFIANCE PRESS
& PUBLISHING

America's Governments: Enemies of the Poor

ISBN-13: 978-1-948035-90-3 (Paperback)
ISBN-13: 978-1-948035-68-2 (eBook)

Edited by Janet Musick
Cover designed by Spomenka Bojanic
Interior designed by Debbi Stocco
Author's photo by Katie Baca of Concord, NH

Published by Defiance Press and Publishing, LLC

Bulk orders of this book may be obtained by contacting Defiance Press and Publishing, LLC at: www.defiancepress.com.

Public Relations Dept. – Defiance Press & Publishing, LLC
281-581-9300
pr@defiancepress.com

Defiance Press & Publishing, LLC
281-581-9300
info@defiancepress.com

Acknowledgements

I AM GRATEFUL TO DANA Wormald, editorial page editor of the Concord (NH) Monitor, for printing my columns regularly from the end of 2016 on. Without Dana's favor all along, this book would not have happened.

Defiance Publishing & Press, and especially its general manager, Heather Siler, also has my gratitude for publishing this book. They were the first publisher I approached. How fortunate for me!

My wife Carolyn, who sadly passed away five years ago, would have been pleased about this book. I appreciate the love and support she gave me.

I am grateful for the concern and support of the wonderful staff of Havenwood-Heritage Heights, the retirement home where I live in Concord, NH.

Thanks also to Katy Delay, who was especially helpful about monetary policy.

My Australian friend, Jim Foran, a fine writer, has made numerous suggestions, large and small. Just his being there, an email away, was a great comfort all along.

ABOUT THE AUTHOR

ARCHIE RICHARDS WAS A STOCKBROKER and financial planner for some years. He then wrote weekly newspaper columns, Richards on Money Matters, which were nationally syndicated. He also authored Understanding Exchange-Traded Funds, published by McGraw-Hill and still available on Amazon. Beginning at the end of 2016, Archie wrote brief libertarian columns about American government that were published as letters by the Concord (NH) Monitor. Those columns, greatly added to, became the basis of this book.

Archie was born in New York City in 1936. After starting work at a Boston bank in 1960, he read the Wall Street Journal and Boston Globe regularly. Having been educated by liberals at St. Paul's School and Yale, he believed himself to be a liberal. Curious about the dynamics of public affairs, however, he cut out articles describing social or economic problems and placed them in a drawer. Several years later, he retrieved the articles and read them again in bulk. It seemed obvious to him that most of the problems were caused by government. Already opposed to the Vietnam War, he became a libertarian in 1968, although that term was then unknown to him.

Archie is also a classical pianist. A recording he made of a famous Beethoven sonata was played on Boston's classical music station on

Sunday morning, October 28, 1973. Even in his eighties, he remains skilled enough to be paid for performances in retirement homes and senior centers in the Boston area.

TABLE OF CONTENTS

FOREWORD

WHEN I STARTED WRITING COLUMNS for the Concord Monitor in December 2016, much of the information came from the Wall Street Journal, which I've spent considerable time reading almost every day for more than half a century. A secondary source was the American Institute for Economic Research (AIER), a reputable organization founded in 1933 to promote limited government and sound money. I went frequently to Google Search to find information from Wikipedia and other sources that seemed trustworthy.

I transcribed information from sources to my columns as best I could. Since I had no book in mind, I did not save all the sources and apologize for this lack of professionalism.

Among the various columns, certain issues may be presented several times. Public affairs, and especially money matters, are complicated. Approaching important issues from different directions makes the knowledge more secure.

Chapter 1 describes 37 ways the U.S. federal, state, and local governments make life harder and more expensive for those with low incomes. Most people are aware of a few damaging policies. But 37? No, people are generally unaware of the enormity of harm.

The issues presented in Chapter 1 are described in shortened form.

Most of those same issues are presented in the same order, but at greater length, in Chapter 3.

Chapter 2 describes the 38th hurt, the most damaging of all: Efforts by the federal government and the Federal Reserve Bank to improve the economy. They fail consistently, as central planning inevitably does for all governments. The result is much greater volatility of the economy. The all-too-frequent economic downturns are devastating for the poor.

Pie-in-the-sky, I would like this book to be a catalyst for cutting spending by America's governments from 37% of the GDP to 10%.

Pamphlets by Thomas Paine in 1776 inspired patriots to fight in America's First Revolution. Who will be the Thomas Paine of America's Second Revolution?

Why, you're reading him right now.

CHAPTER 1 – 37 WAYS U.S. GOVERNMENTS HURT THE POOR

NOTE: Squeezed in just before publication, a crucial column describing the essence of modern liberalism is properly placed at the beginning of Chapter 8. I mention it here because of its importance.

U.S. FEDERAL, STATE, AND LOCAL governments make life harder and more expensive for those with low incomes. Most people are probably aware of one or two damaging policies. But 37? No, people are generally unaware of the enormity of damage.

The issues presented in this chapter are described in shortened form. Chapter 3 presents the same issues in the same order, but at greater length.

Nothing is harder on the poor than serious economic downturns. These have resulted from efforts by the government and the Federal Reserve Bank to improve the economy – efforts that cannot help but fail. The faulty attempts I'm aware of are detailed in Chapter 2 and are not counted among the 37 summarized here.

POLICIES THAT HURT THE POOR

Government Lotteries trigger gambling addictions and breed poverty. States advertise aggressively in poor areas, encouraging people to treat lotteries as investments, not entertainment. In effect, government lotteries are regressive taxes.

Occupational Licenses: Nearly a quarter of Americans require occupational licenses to do their jobs. The licenses require fees and long periods of training that people with low incomes cannot afford. People in an occupation lobby government to keep others out. The resulting shortage of workers raises prices, causing the poor to be hit twice: They are unable to attain the licensed jobs, and also pay higher prices for their purchases.

Rent Control: When building restrictions cause apartments to be in short supply, rents rise. State and local governments therefore impose rent control, which requires landlords to keep the rent payments level for as long as the tenant remains in the apartment, despite the landlord's rising costs. The beneficiaries are older, relatively prosperous tenants whose lives are stable. The rent can be raised to market levels only when the tenant vacates. Younger, less-prosperous people who move frequently therefore face higher rents.

Minimum Wages: The hourly labor of some of the poorly educated is worth less than the minimum wage. Minimum wage laws prevent them from being hired. But the average person subject to minimum wage, including wives of working husbands and youths still at home, lives in a household with total income of more than $50,000. The laws do little good, but cause substantial harm.

Rich, Powerful, and Relatively Independent Unions could not exist in their present form without the federal laws that support them. The wages of union members are forced unnaturally high by union pressure, raising everyone's costs. The poor, who are generally not union members but spend most of their income on living expenses, are the most affected.

The War on Drugs has been longer, more costly, and more damaging than was the prohibition of alcohol in the 1920s. The criminalization of drugs causes their prices to rise, attracting suppliers who are willing to disobey the law. Supply increases, and this stimulates higher demand. Suppliers of illegal drugs enforce their property rights with violence, most of which occurs in poor areas.

Food Subsidies: The U.S. Farm Bill of 1973 and its successors pay billions of dollars annually to prosperous farmers who produce staple commodities, especially corn. Around the same year, 1973, obesity began to develop in America. Obesity is a leading cause of premature deaths. More than a quarter of the population is now obese. The foods causing the obesity are the very ones receiving federal subsidies. They are also the cheapest, causing the poor to be affected disproportionately.

Crony Capitalism: When government is big, the rich gain wealth faster than the poor because they induce government to help them.

Government Welfare creates dependency and hinders recipients from obtaining jobs. Say a woman who receives $200 a week from welfare is offered $300 a week from a 40-hour-a-week job. The job would terminate her welfare, however, making her effective income rise by only $100 a week, or $2.50 an hour. She chooses to remain on welfare. Private welfare organizations would deal more sensitively with such problems.

Anti-Prostitution: Some low-income women need prostitution to support themselves, but without being considered criminals. It is only in illegal industries that participants are mistreated and held against their will. Once legalized, prostitutes would eventually be esteemed and could hold their heads high for performing a valuable service.

High Regulatory Costs of Child Care: Heavy regulations in some states have made the costs of child care exorbitant, making it nearly impossible for single, low-income parents to obtain jobs outside the home. Officials disregard the financial strain. Child care should be left to the people and free markets to solve.

Price Controls on Interest Rates: For many years, the Federal Reserve Bank has kept interest rates unnaturally low. Banks lend to the rich because the risk is low and repayment seems assured. But they're less likely to lend to the non-rich, because the low interest returns may not match the higher risks. This widens the gap between rich and poor.

Houses, like automobiles, cost more than they're worth when they're new and less than they're worth when they're used. The prosperous overpay to build houses. When they vacate, the less prosperous would underpay to move in, transferring enormous value from rich to poor. This huge, unintentional, non-governmental, income-transfer program is prevented from operating because government intrudes so heavily in real estate markets.

Government Subsidies cause people to arrange their affairs to obtain them, and the changes are usually not in the nation's best interests. When offered a subsidy, for example, businesses tend to replace engineers with lawyers. (This matter is not enlarged upon in Chapter 3.)

Social Security Inequities: Social Security benefits terminate when a person dies. The life expectancy of black men is significantly shorter than the life expectancy of white women. Therefore, the Social Security (FICA) taxes paid by black men support the lives of white women, but not the other way around.

Anti-Gouging Laws: Forcing down the prices of products during emergencies reduces the supply of the product, especially in poor areas.

Lockdowns hurt the poor more than the rich. This issue is discussed in some detail in Chapter 4.

POLICIES THAT HURT EVERYONE

Since the poor spend most of their income on living costs, policies that hurt everyone affect them the most:

- **Healthcare:** With the first dollars of healthcare costs paid by insurance companies or government, as they are now, consumers have little need to inquire about costs. Healthcare costs are therefore approximately double what they should be. If health-care consumers paid all of their healthcare costs each year up to the amount of a reasonable deductible on their insurance policy, they would take great interest in healthcare prices. The competition among suppliers would drive costs down. All costs above the deductibles would be covered by inexpensive catastrophic insurance policies.

- **Taxing the Rich** at high progressive tax rates does not help the poor. The prosperous do not spend all their income, but the excess does not go under their mattresses. The excess may be invested directly in a business. Or it may be deposited in a CD or a money market fund, from which it's lent out for others to invest in businesses. Wherever the money goes, it indirectly generates jobs. The income earned by a low-income person exceeds the income he would have received in welfare, and of course the job also improves his morale. The higher the percentage of income of a prosperous person that's taken by the government, the less she has available to generate activity in the private sector. It's the private sector that generates wealth, not the government.

- **Political Professionalism:** Regardless of party, the longer members of Congress remain in office, the more they favor big government. House and Senate members should be limited to one term each, with their pay significantly reduced. People running for office would not expect to remain for long. It would be "their turn to serve." The pressure to appease interest groups would be sharply reduced. Instead of creating new government programs, members could focus on getting rid of the damaging old ones.

- **Zoning** impedes the operation of a free market economy. Without it, factories would not be built in residential areas, because residential land is too expensive. Despite having no zoning, Houston, Texas, has thrived. Zoning has been particularly hard on residents of California.

- **Regulations:** In 2018, federal bureaucrats issued eleven regulations for every law passed by Congress. The estimated annual cost of compliance, $1.9 trillion, was greater than corporate and personal income tax revenues combined. The estimated annual cost to each U.S. household, on average, was at least $14,600.

- **Bank Deposit Insurance** induces depositors to care about a bank's interest rate and convenience, but not the money's safety. The guarantees have made possible the enormous expansion of debt throughout the economy. Without those guarantees, big depositors would have found ways to assure the safety of their money, reducing the nation's level of debt and benefiting everyone.

- **Davis-Bacon:** Contractors must pay construction workers on federally funded jobs "local prevailing wages." This artificially inflates the wages of construction workers and requires an army of bureaucrats to enforce its measures. It also substantially raises the prices paid by travelers and consumers for the public works they utilize.

- **College Education** has deteriorated as the federal government funneled enormous funds to colleges and also subsidized and guaranteed student loans. Despite the subsidies, the colleges raised tuitions anyway, building elaborate student centers and hiring thousands of administrators. College was made less accessible to the poor.

- **Tariffs:** Tariffs are taxes, and they weaken the economy. Whatever is taxed you get less of. If steel is subject to tariffs, you get less steel for the money. For years, Hong Kong imposed no tariffs on products it imported, even when opposing countries imposed tariffs on Hong Kong products they imported. It's no coincidence that Hong Kong has had, for decades, the fastest growing economy in the world.

- **Drug Testing:** All drug testing should be performed by the private sector. Since government has no profits, bureaucrats give high priority to the avoidance of blame and tend to keep effective drugs off the market longer than necessary. More lives have been lost because of the delays than have been saved by the government assuring itself that the drugs are safe and effective.

- **Flood Insurance:** The government sets flood insurance premiums unrealistically low. The benefits are substantial and obvious for seacoast dwellers. The per capita costs are hidden for the Americans who pay a few extra pennies of taxes. People of low income who can't afford coastline real estate pay the costs but gain no benefit from the faulty policy.

- **The Jones Act** requires that goods shipped between U.S. ports and territories must be carried on ships built in America, 75% owned and crewed by Americans, with the shipped goods never sold to foreign citizens. The act was supposed to protect U.S. shipping. But plenty of shipping to and from the U.S. has been protected out of existence. Repealing the law and using cheaper foreign-made ships would increase the volume of ships operating in U.S. waters, stimulating the economy.

- **Price Controls on Products:** The federal government keeps the prices of sugar, citrus, and other products higher than the world prices. The beneficiaries are the few companies that supply the products, while the per capita costs paid by the rest of Americans are small. The benefits to the few are large and obvious. The costs to the many are small and hidden.

- **Postal Service:** The 630,000 U.S. postal employees are the world's highest-paid, semi-skilled workers. The price of a one-ounce, first-class letter is currently 55 cents, whether it's sent across the street or 7,894 miles from Concord, NH to Guam. This is crazy! Prices should be set according to costs. Technology is rendering postal services obsolescent. Emails we can send for free. Covering the increasing postal deficits with taxes or piling them onto the federal deficit is outrageous. Privatizing the postal service would save a bundle.

Harmful Policies Many Consider Unthinkable to Reverse

- **Schools:** Government should neither educate nor fund the education of anyone at any level. All schools should be owned by individuals, associations, or corporations, with or without profits. With income tax rates reduced, prosperous citizens would help pay the costs of inner city schools.

- **Global Warming** predictions have consistently been exaggerated. The computer models of proponents are guesses, not scientific fact, and can readily be manipulated. The politicization of science stems from the personal income of scientists coming directly or indirectly from the federal government. Soon, advancing technology will replace industries that produce CO_2 emissions with those that don't. Fears about global warming are way overdone, and the unnecessary costs are enormous. (Other columns on this issue appear in Chapter 6.)

- **The Deep State:** The Pendleton Civil Service Reform Act of 1883 created a permanent, merit-based bureaucracy that now numbers 2.8 million individuals whose salaries and benefits greatly exceed those of people with equivalent private sector jobs. Collectively, deep state members indirectly influence policies to increase their budgets, increase their power over others, and avoid blame. It's an indirect but massive form of corruption. Today's bureaucracy is far more damaging than that of the former spoils system. It's time to trash the Civil Service and drain the swamp.

- **The National Debt,** already higher than the year's gross domestic product, cannot accumulate indefinitely. Current Americans blithely expect future Americans to limit *their* consumption to repay it. But future Americans will be unwilling to bear the brunt of our current profligacy. If the debt continues to grow faster than the economy, the federal government will eventually go bankrupt. Runaway inflation would make savings, Social Security, and Medicare payments worthless. Banks and insurance companies would go under. Widespread bankruptcy would prevail, and consumption would fall sharply, hurting the poor most. Blame would likely fall heavily on the Jews. Is there a happier scenario? Yes. See page 83 for more information.

Governments Should Sell Land They Own but Do Not Themselves Occupy: Forests, rivers, mountains, parks, prairies, reservoirs, aquifers, swamps, deserts, tundra, and national parks should be auctioned to the highest bidders. About 80% of Nevada and 60% of Utah would go. The management of these lands would improve, and costs would decline.

Interstates, Bridges, and Streets should be sold to the highest bidders. Technology will enable owners to know who is using their roads, enabling them to charge users accordingly. Trucking companies would be properly charged for road deterioration, reducing the costs for everyone else. More goods would be carried on long hauls by privatized rail, which is cheaper than using trucks.

Chapter 2 – The Biggest Hurt

THE BIGGEST HURT TO AMERICAN citizens, but especially the poor, are the severe economic contractions that throw people out of work. The contractions are invariably caused by the federal government and the Federal Reserve Bank. The federal government should stop all interference with the economy. The Federal Reserve Bank should be abolished.

Government's efforts to improve the economy only make it worse. Its intrusions interfere with free pricing. Information the government relies on is always out of date and less reliable than information the economy supplies itself with more than a billion transactions a day, enabling the economy to improve without help. The counterintuitive effects of government's economic interventions are especially powerful.

Here are severe economic downturns that have hurt American citizens deeply, especially the poor:

The Great Depression: Government and Federal Reserve Bank policies caused, lengthened, and intensified the Great Depression. Unemployment reached 24.9%. Among many other intrusions, the Hoover administration increased tariffs and income tax rates. Government prevented chain stores from passing on to customers the savings from big volume purchases. At government's urging, employers paid their employees high wages but were forced to lay off millions of workers. During Franklin D. Roosevelt's administration, anti-business rhetoric and numerous antitrust suits disrupted the economy. The dollar was devalued, creating chaos and voiding innumerable contracts. Businesses were told how much to produce, how much to charge, and where to sell. The Federal Reserve first expanded the money supply to excess and then reduced it drastically after the downturn had begun.

During the 1970s, federal expenditures increased enormously. The top rate for long-term capital gains was an economy-killing 70%. The high telephone prices of AT&T, a government-imposed monopoly, raised everyone's costs. Millions of prices charged by railroads, airlines, and natural gas companies were set too low by the government, interfering with the economy's normal workings. Regulators forced truckers to keep costs high, thereby protecting the established companies from competition. Generalized wage and price controls were imposed. The Federal Reserve created an excess of money, raising prices and interest rates. Under Regulation Q, the Fed also imposed ceilings on the rates banks could pay for deposits. But inflation pushed interest rates higher than the ceilings, causing depositors to withdraw billions of dollars from banks, squeezing the economy dry.

The 2008 Credit Crisis and Subsequent Great Recession: A detailed explanation of the causes of the 2008 Credit Crisis appears later in this chapter.

Current Monetary Policies: Congress requires the Federal Reserve to maintain price stability and maximum sustainable employment. No one can do both at the same time. High unemployment being more politically sensitive, the Fed generally gives priority to this and makes price stability secondary. An item costing one dollar in 1913, when the Federal Reserve Bank was created, would cost about $26 today, a poor performance. Overwrought about deflation, the Fed seems unaware that deflation caused by a plentiful supply of goods is appropriate and healthy. The Fed's wild fluctuations of the money supply and its manipulations of foreign currencies increase economic volatility, which is especially hard on low-income Americans. The government should impose a gold standard so that entrepreneurs can feel more assured about their capital investments. Better yet, the Federal Reserve should be terminated altogether. Anything should serve as legal currency. As long as each currency can be freely exchanged for every other, the ones that best hold their value and are most convenient would be retained. The others would be discarded. For years, Europeans accommodated the use of several currencies. When a financial crisis calls for extra liquidity, private parties would supply it better and more promptly than government.

I expect a significant increase in the rate of inflation during the next few years. Any such increase would probably surprise the hapless Fed.

(Government estimates of what an item bought in 1913 would cost today are mentioned several times in this book. The estimates vary somewhat because the columns were written at different times.)

ELIMINATE THE FEDERAL RESERVE BANK

November 20, 2017. The Federal Reserve Bank will probably have a new chairman, Jerome Powell. The best thing he could do is close the place down.

Authorized by the Constitution to regulate the value of money, Congress has delegated the matter to the Federal Reserve Bank, requiring it to maintain price stability and maximum sustainable employment. No one can do both at the same time. Since high unemployment is more obvious than price instability, the Fed strives for low unemployment (which itself is impossible for any central bank to achieve) and makes price stability secondary.

How stable have those prices been? Let's see: An item costing one dollar in 1913, when the Federal Reserve was created, would cost $24.92 today. For this sorry record, you can credit the Fed's poor monetary management and no gold backing.

In the 1930s, the Fed reduced the money supply by about a third. This would have been okay if done slowly, years earlier. But the rapid decline after the Depression had started brought substantial price drops and widespread bankruptcy.

The Fed is now overwrought about deflation. A rapid decline of the money supply can bring severe problems, as described just above. But deflation caused by the increased supply of goods, as is occurring now in prosperous Switzerland, does not.

Stable prices are obtained by a steady increase in the amount of money, backed by gold. For this, the Federal Reserve's enormous bureaucracy would be unnecessary.

The Fed's wild fluctuations of the money supply and manipulations of foreign currencies have increased economic volatility and unemployment and suppressed economic growth, all of which have been especially hard on low-income Americans.

No one can consistently predict the economy, especially not government officials. The Federal Reserve's attempts have failed.

The Fed has tried to regulate the economy by controlling interest rates. This hasn't worked. In the long run, price controls never work. For the last decade, interest rates have been kept unnaturally low. This has not only deprived savers of reasonable returns, it has also widened the gap between rich and poor. Even though the interest returns are low, banks are still willing to lend to the rich because the risk is low. Banks are less willing to lend to small businesses and common folks because the low interest returns do not offset the higher risks.

The Federal Reserve Bank should be eliminated. Sorry, but any organization with 400 PhD economists on staff is likely to be wrong most of the time.

THE 2008 CREDIT CRISIS WAS
CAUSED BY GOVERNMENT[1]

March 26, 2018. We're approaching the tenth anniversary of the 2008 Credit Crisis, which brought years of financial havoc. The Dow fell 54%. The unemployment rate more than doubled to 10%. It's true that banks and financial companies lowered their ethical standards, but this was induced by government requirements. The primary causes of the downturn were the following federal policies:

Since 1933, the Federal Deposit Insurance Corporation has insured bank deposits. All deposit guarantees are a mistake. They induce depositors to care about a bank's interest rate and convenience, but not the money's safety. The guarantees enabled debt to expand for decades throughout the economy. Without them, big depositors would have insisted on the safety of their money, reducing the nation's level of debt.

Beginning in the late-1990s, the Federal Reserve Bank expanded the money supply and lowered interest rates to excess. Increasing government regulations discouraged business investments. People bought real estate instead, and real estate prices soared.

In 2004, the Securities and Exchange Commission authorized five banks to accumulate unlimited debt. Previously, all banks had been required to restrict their debts to twelve times their assets. But Merrill Lynch, Lehman Brothers, and Bear Stearns, with their borrowings unlimited, all failed, their debts having risen up to forty times their assets.

By 2005, the Community Reinvestment Act had forced banks to lend at least 52% of their available mortgage money to people with low income. Regulators threatened to put banks that didn't comply out of business, and the regulators were deadly serious about it. To meet the requirement, banks had to make frenetic efforts to find sufficient numbers of low-income borrowers and therefore had to disregard potentially

---

1. I spent considerable time researching all this from many sources on the Web.

fraudulent loan applications. Ethical standards do not change quickly without provocation. The government's outrageous 52% requirement was just such a provocation. It forced banks to lower their underwriting standards.

Fannie Mae and Freddie Mac were sponsored by the government to bundle groups of mortgages and sell them as mortgage bonds to investors. This allowed loan originators to sell older loans and reinvest by offering new ones. In the early 2000s, the government also authorized higher-risk loans and urged companies to make such loans. The number of mortgages soared. Enormous profits ensued, especially since Fannie Mae and Freddie Mac had low borrowing costs due to widespread assumptions that the government would guarantee their loans. Other banks, with higher borrowing costs, competed by increasing the risks of their mortgage loans and securities. Large congressional campaign contributions helped the industry grow in size and risk. It would have been safer if an unlimited number of mortgage bundlers had competed with one another with no government involvement.

Standard & Poor's, Moody's, and Fitch were authorized by the government as the nation's principal evaluators of bonds. The government's earnestness about expanding home ownership and the widespread expectation of real estate prices rising induced the three agencies to rate many mortgage bonds, including sub-primes, with the highest triple-A rating. Again, it would have been safer if an unlimited number of bond evaluators had competed with one another with no government involvement.

The Mark-to-Market Rule, part of the Sarbanes-Oxley Act, required banks to value their mortgage loans and other assets for what they could be sold for almost immediately. It was as if your house had to be sold by day's end. After the credit crisis hit in 2008, the mortgage assets held by banks traded hardly at all, making reasonable valuations impossible. Banks had to lower their asset values way down, reducing lending substantially. The Mark-to-Market Rule was repealed in April of 2009, but not before great damage was done.[2]

After the 2008 bankruptcy of Lehman Brothers, the Federal Reserve required banks to raise their capital from 4% of assets to 7%. With the credit crisis having already begun, banks couldn't raise capital in public markets. They had to reduce their loan assets instead. During the next two years, commercial bank loans fell by 25%, the largest such reduction since the Great Depression.[3]

These eight federal policies caused the 2008 credit crisis and the economic travails that followed. As with all serious economic downturns, the people hurt most were the poor.

THE FEDERAL RESERVE BANK'S CONCEIT

September 24, 2018. The Federal Reserve Bank continues to fail in its efforts to control the economy.

But first, for readers who aren't familiar with bonds, here's a brief explanation:

A bond is a promise to pay a certain amount at a certain date and a promise to pay specific interest payments in the interim. Bonds can be bought and sold all along the way. Whoever owns the bond when an interest payment is made receives the interest. Whoever owns the bond at maturity receives the final interest payment and the repayment of the principal.

The interest payments and the final principal payment remain fixed. This means that if the price of the bond falls, the fixed interest and principal payments bulk larger in terms of the price paid, causing the *yield* of the bond to rise. Price down. Yield up. The price and yield of bonds move

---

2. Steve Forbes discussed many of these issues in Forbes editorials. He was especially eloquent about the devastating Mark-to-Market Rule. Such a high level of government ignorance makes me angry!
3. Ditto!

in opposite directions.

If the price of the bond rises, the fixed interest and principal payments diminish in terms of the price paid, causing the yield of the bond to fall. Price up. Yield down. The price and yield of bonds move...well, you're on top of that.

For the first time in interest rate history, the prices of many long-term bonds have risen so much that the costs for buying the bonds overwhelm the fixed interest payments, causing the yields to be negative. Price way up. Yield way down to *negative* numbers. In effect, buyers don't receive a return on the bonds; they pay for the right to own them. Why do they put up with this? Perhaps because they can't think of anything else to do with their money that has relatively low risk.

Did you get all that? Doesn't matter if you didn't.

Okay, back to my story. To fund long-term investments, companies often borrow the money with long-term bonds. The prices of long-term bonds are the most important prices in the entire economy. The prices should be set by supply and demand. But they're not. The Federal Reserve Bank indirectly controls them. Government price controls are always harmful. In its conceit, the Fed picks the most important price to control. No one knows how much economic disruption this causes.

Business leaders are more willing to make long-term investments when they feel assured that the dollar's value will remain level. In 1913, when the Federal Reserve was created, an item bought for $1.00 would cost $25.46 today. How's that for monetary stability?

The Fed's wild fluctuations of the U.S. money supply and its manipulations of foreign currencies increase economic volatility. The Fed's top-down planning has caused serious economic downturns that would not have occurred had the government simply imposed a gold standard to preserve the value of the dollar. Economies work better when they're self-guided, not by government, but by personal liberty, supply and demand, free pricing, competition, and a level value of the currency.

The Federal Reserve Bank and the federal government itself are responsible for numerous economic downturns. The citizens hurt most are the poor.

THE LURCHING FED[4]

June 2, 2020. The controlling Board of the Federal Reserve Bank numbers seven people. Their pretensions are insufferable, and they pay no penalty for being wrong.

In 2008, the Credit Crisis hit the financial sector hard. The Fed didn't see it coming and didn't realize they'd helped cause it.

The economy was in a pickle. Whoops, we've got a problem here, they noted. The economy can't recover from this without our help. Certainly not.

They engaged in what they called "Quantitative Easing," which is a euphemism for throwing their weight around. They bought Treasury securities and mortgage-backed securities, and created new money to pay for them, thereby expanding the Fed's balance sheet from $1 trillion to $4 trillion.

Four *trillion* dollars! That's the equivalent of a year's economic production of the 83 million people of Germany! Only four nations have GDPs larger than Germany's: Japan, China, and the United States.

But wait a minute. Flooding the American economy with an extra $3 trillion threatened big-time inflation. Whoops, we're got a problem here. We've got to soak up some of that extra money.

The Fed thus began paying interest on funds deposited by banks with the Fed, stimulating the banks to increase their Fed deposits enormously. The interest paid by the Fed represented profit to the banks.

4. WSJ, Andy Kessler, *The Fed Can't See Its Own Shadow*, 9/9/19, and WSJ, Judy Shelton, *The Case for Monetary Regime Change*, 4/22/19. Neither Kessler nor Shelton suggested eliminating the Fed. This requires someone who may be angrier and less circumspect than they are. WSJ, Phil Gramm and Mike Solon, *Why the Fed May Not Duck Inflation This Time*, 5/29/20.

With the economy diminished by the credit crisis, the demand for loans was weak.

Apart from the Fed, but probably because of Fed interventions, the banks of the world have created a shadow-banking system that I don't understand well enough to describe to you. But it's huge, and it has caused a shortage of long-term Treasury bonds, which is one reason why the interest rates on long bonds are lower than they have ever been in 4,000 years of interest rate history.

Seven people. Demi-gods they're not. They base their actions on information dug up by 400 PhD economists and 20,000 other people on the staff. This information is infinitesimal in comparison with the information the economy supplies itself from more than a billion free-market transactions a day – information that would enable the economy to cure itself remarkably quickly if the government just kept its hands off.

Lurching from one policy to another, having no idea of the long-term consequences of their actions, throwing around money equal to the GDP of Germany, those seven know-it-alls with no skin in the game go on and on bringing harm to America. It's preposterous!

Right from the start, in 1913, the Fed has been wrong far more often than right. The economic downturns it has precipitated have been hardest on the poor. For the economy to be more stable, healthier, and more egalitarian, the Fed must be eliminated. The sooner the better.

THE BOGUS PHILLIPS CURVE

August 30, 2020. For years, the Federal Reserve has operated on the assumption that unemployment rates and inflation rates move in opposite directions. The theory is called the Phillips Curve.

When unemployment is high (which is bad), economic weakness supposedly causes inflation to be low. The theory goes that to bring the unemployment rate down, the Fed needs to increase inflation.

When inflation is high (which is bad), the strong economy supposedly reduces unemployment. To bring the inflation rate down, the Fed needs to weaken the economy a bit and allow unemployment to rise.

Steve Forbes, who knows more about monetary policy in his sleep than members of the Federal Reserve Board do when they're awake, has said for years that the Phillips Curve is bogus. Well, the Fed has finally been forced to face facts. It now acknowledges that, prior to the pandemic anyway, both unemployment and inflation plummeted to rock bottom levels at the same time.

The Fed has not announced what it plans to do now. Whatever the plan, it will prove misguided.

The Fed has been guided by the Phillips Curve and other misconceptions for years. The Soviet Union was guided by its five-year plans. The economy has no plan. It simply adjusts. It adjusts for changes in every cubic millimeter of space, nature, and things. It adjusts for changes in the character, inclinations, and capabilities of every person. It makes separate adjustments everywhere during every millisecond of time. What can a lumbering central planner do except disrupt, leaving us all worse off?

ECONOMIC GROWTH AND GOVERNMENT SPENDING[5]

An article published by the American Institute for Economic Research reveals a key relationship between government spending and economic growth.

The study extends for 150 years, divided into three periods of fifty years each – long enough to level out short-term changes.

The first period, the "Gilded Age," extends from 1868, near the end of the Civil War, to 1917, near the end of World War I. Federal spending each year during that time averaged a low 2.5% of the Gross Domestic

---

5. AIER, Richard M. Salsman *As the U.S. Government Grows, American Prosperity Slows,* 5/21/19.

Product (GDP). The economy, as measured by the Industrial Production Index, grew at a sizzling 4.9% per year.

The second period, extended from 1918 to 1967, encompasses the Great Depression and World War II. Federal spending averaged 14.3% of the GDP each year (up substantially from 2.5% above). The economy grew at a slower pace: 3.9% per year (down from 4.9%). Clearly, the more government spending, the slower the growth.

During the final period, from 1968 to 2018, federal spending soared, averaging 22.1% of GDP. Yikes! The economy grew at an abysmal pace, averaging a mere 2.1% a year.

Liberals would say there are other ingredients to the slowing of growth besides government growth.

Really? What are they? Certainly government's growth is by far the most important.

Maybe so, but the government helped make the prosperity more equal.

It did no such thing. Government has reduced America's equality. Big government slows economic growth with no compensating benefits.

PRICE CONTROLS ON LONG-TERM BONDS

Government price controls are always a bad idea. When government forces down the price of a product, buyers sense a bargain, and the demand increases. But the people who supply the product make too little money, and they reduce the supply.

High demand. Low supply. Obvious imbalance. After the price control is lifted, as it must be eventually, the price pops up to higher levels than would have prevailed had the price control not been imposed in the first place.

The most important price in the entire economy, the interest rate on long-term bonds, is controlled by the Federal Reserve Bank. (How it does this is beyond the scope of this book.)

Companies look far ahead when they plan new mines, new factories, new hospitals, new transportation equipment, and everything that goes with those capital goods. The bulk of the money to pay for all this is borrowed, which for companies often means selling long-term bonds.

When the Federal Reserve Bank keeps the interest rate on long-term bonds too low (and the price too high), the companies planning their long-term capital goods say, "Whoopee! Let's go for it."

But people who supply the money say, "I'm lending you my money for several decades, and you're paying me that piddling amount of interest? The heck with it; I'll put my money elsewhere."

Eventually, the controls have to be lifted, and the interest rate is likely to rise higher than would have prevailed had the controls not been imposed in the first place.

GOVERNMENT: PULL BACK THIS TIME[6]

The U.S. economy plummeted after World War I, with unemployment around 20%. Few people now are aware of this crash, because it ended so quickly. President Warren Harding knocked off his card games and slashed spending, cut tax rates, and reduced regulations. (With presidents, what counts are the person's policies, not his character.) The economy rebounded, launching the economic innovations of the 1920s.

In 1929, American suffered another little downturn. It lasted more than a decade, and we certainly know about that one. Herbert Hoover was an engineer of exemplary character, enormous capability, and miserable policies. He sought to engineer a better economy, but brought on a severe depression instead. Together with Congress, Hoover raised tariffs and income tax rates substantially, created a bevy of new bureaucracies, imposed onerous regulations, and incurred high government expen-

---

6. Forbes, Steve Forbes, *Less Can Be More – Much More,* May 2020.

ditures. Franklin D. Roosevelt ("I don't know what I think until I hear myself talk.") imposed similar big government policies, extending and intensifying the Great Depression.

Many feared an economic decline after World War II. But President Truman (my favorite Democrat; I bet if he read this book, he'd switch parties), slashed spending, sharply lowered tariffs, lowered tax rates, and cancelled numerous regulations. Even though millions of veterans joined the workforce at the time, unemployment remained low.

We face another depression now. President Trump has cut tax rates and cancelled numerous damaging regulations. But he gives every sign of being a big spender. This characterization certainly applies to members of both parties in Congress.

Mr. Trump campaigned on draining the swamp. That's impossible without big spending cuts, especially of entitlements. Let's hope he wasn't putting us on. After the excessive stimulus packages, the government must cut its spending, preferably to the bone. If it doesn't, the American government will go broke.

GOLD STANDARD

August 26, 2019. America should adopt a gold standard for its currency.

This means the government would define its money in terms of a fixed weight of gold. For example, it might set the price at $1,200 an ounce and keep it there. Anyone could exchange dollars for gold or gold for dollars at that price indefinitely.

To keep the price of gold from rising and keep the nation from losing its gold to other nations, the government would restrict the creation of money to about the pace of population growth.

This is why today's liberals consider a gold standard a wretched idea. They prefer the current free-wheeling procedures, and they want no restrictions on their use of power. They keep their blinders on tightly to avoid seeing the miserable results.

Back to my story. A level value of the currency would stimulate economic growth. When companies sink their money into the development of capital goods that won't pay off for years, the companies want to feel assured that the value of the money they will eventually receive has roughly the same purchasing power as the money originally invested.

Making no predictions and setting no interest rates, the central bank should let the economy take care of itself, simply assuring the currency's convertibility to gold at the statutory price. The level value of the dollar would result in faster economic growth and less economic volatility, helping the poor most.

The Federal Reserve Bank should stop trying to predict the future. Most of the time, they've been wrong. The biggest decline of a generation started in 2008. The Fed didn't see it coming and, in fact, partly caused it. The Fed's staff should adopt new careers and do something helpful to society for a change.

Advanced computers have made almost all central banks believe they can forecast the future. Most have failed, resulting in excessive debts and inflation worldwide.

HOW TO MAKE THE ECONOMY LESS VOLATILE

The poor are devastated by serious economy downturns. Nothing would help them more than to make the economy less volatile.

Reasonably stable economic growth with increasing living standards across all income levels is most likely to occur when the value of its currency is stable.

Left to itself, with little government involvement, the economy would achieve relative stability. Nothing's perfect, of course. But when the economy gets out of whack, it corrects itself before long. With government involved, the economy gets whackier and whackier.

For example, I recall that, during the late 1970s, the Federal Reserve Bank created a tremendous amount of new money. Other government impediments made entrepreneurs reluctant to start new businesses. The extra money was used to speculate in real estate, where prices soared. Bureaucrats at the Department of Agriculture, just as bullish about real estate as everyone else, urged farmers to buy as much land as they could. When the bubble burst, many farms failed. Not a single bureaucrat was fired.

The people who work for government, in case you were wondering, are people. They have biases, likes and dislikes. When most of Americans are excited about real estate and think prices are sure to rise, the people who work for government are likely to think so too. But unlike everyone else, they have the power of coercion, which means the damage caused by their being wrong is multiplied.

As explained above, the government's numerous intrusions resulted in the Credit Crisis of 2008. Government was also largely responsible for the Great Depression and the significant bear market of 1974.

At times, the government has handed out money to people on the assumption that money stimulates prosperity. The government is wrong about this. Dollar stimulants do not create value. They simply diminish the value of the currency and cause healthy economic growth to falter. Heaven help us, the diminishment of growth is especially powerful if the government payments people receive when not working are greater than the pay they would receive if they returned to work.

Money feels like wealth, but it is not. You can create a product or a service, which is indeed wealth. If you use it yourself, this adds to your wealth but involves no money. You can sell your product or service to someone else. This brings in money, which stores the value of the wealth you created for your use in the future. You can, of course, exchange the money for a product or service created by someone else. But it is always the product or service that's the wealth, not the money. The money sim-

ply stores value over time and across borders. When the government hands out money, it believes it is distributing wealth. Not so, which is why the economy usually does not come alive after such distributions.

Why does economic volatility and diminished value of the currency cause healthy economic growth to falter? Because companies plan far ahead. It often takes years before capital goods actually come into being and start generating profits. If companies fear that the profits won't be realized or the value of the dollar will deteriorate during those years, they may decide not to create the capital goods to begin with.

Healthy economic growth occurs when economy volatility is mild and when the value of the currency remains a reliable unit of account and store of value. But money should not only store value, it should also *preserve* value. This requires the creators of money to avoid producing too much of it.

The Federal Reserve Bank was created in 1913, supposedly to prevent heavy volatility in the economy and in the value of the dollar. It has failed. It has created anything but a stable monetary system.

Are you with me so far? I try to write about economics so clearly that even *I* understand it.

Okay. Here's how economic volatility can be mild:

Government must take its hands off the tiller and let the economy alone. Government central planning cannot help but fail. Three hundred million people going about their business affect the prices of the goods and services they use. We're talking about more than a billion transactions a day, including the ones behind the scenes, like the payments businesses make to each other and futures prices on commodities. Every price is a signal of supply and demand. Successful central planners would have to know them all. They would also have to know the personality and knowledge of every person, minute details on consumer demand, the production processes of every producer, not to mention detailed

knowledge of all the other persons and economies of the world.[7]

The Fed's information is infinitesimal in comparison. They're making intuitive guesses, even though the results of most government policies are counterintuitive.

Of course, we can't impose any system that forces government to toe the line and keep its hands off the economy. Government is bigger and more powerful than anyone else. All we have is the ballot box. When elected officials meddle with the economy, they should be thrown the hell out of office.

An economy whose growth is relatively steady and equitable also requires a favorable monetary system. I believe a monetary system is best when it is delegated to the people. The Federal Reserve Bank and its staff of more than 20,000 people do more harm than good. They should be fired and the place closed down.

Any bank or any nation that creates a currency makes a profit from that currency. It costs the U.S. government about 12.3 cents to manufacture a $100 dollar bill. But it sells the bill for one hundred smackers. Talk about easy money! The profit potential is called "seigniorage." Governments love that seigniorage and hate to give it up.

But anyone can create a currency. Other than governments, the organizations most likely to do the job well are banks. Most of the money we use is not cash; it consists of bank deposits, which are all electronic. If everyone tried to turn their bank accounts into green cash, the amount of cash available would fall short by far more than 90%. Banks and the government create bank accounts electronically. The only cost is the salary of the person who pushes a button on the bank's computer. Bingo, there's a million new dollars, all profit. Nice work if you can get it. But the next day, the bank might have to diminish the number of dollars by a million – that's the way it goes.

---

7. AIER, David Hart, *Pandemic Policy in One Page*, 5/29/20. This paragraph also encapsulates a cardinal view of Austrian economist and Nobel Prize winner Friedrich von Hayek.

I now present a monetary system different from the gold standard, whereby government delegates the monetary system altogether to the people:

The government would relinquish its monopoly over the U.S. dollar. The government could still produce dollars, but citizens could use other currencies as well, such as CitiDollars, BancAmericaDollars, gold, pounds, marks, yen, cigarettes, or anything else. Cigarettes are sometimes used in prisons as money, but of course they're too flimsy for wider use. Pebbles have been used in some societies but they're much too inconvenient. People would accommodate to having many currencies. Europeans did so for years.

Each currency would be convertible into every other in markets unfettered by government control. The currencies compete with one another. The public would choose those that are most convenient and best hold their value. The others would be disregarded. Creators try to avoid their currency being disregarded because they would lose their seigniorage.

Elsewhere in this book, I have recommended a gold standard, which is far better than the seat-of-the-pants monetary system we have now. But somebody in government has to set the gold price, and they likely will do it incorrectly.

Instead, the government should release its monopoly on the dollar and allow many currencies to compete with one another. This approach would enable us to get rid of the Federal Reserve Bank altogether.

If government is no longer involved with the monetary system, and the FDIC no longer exists, banks would have the incentive to be cautious. They wouldn't want to be left holding the bag

when people go bankrupt. They would make collateralized loans on the basis of specific plans. When the plans are realized, the loans would be repaid. The most desirable loans are those that are repaid in gold. People who have accumulated too much debt could go bankrupt, limiting the amount the bank is repaid.

Generally, currency creators would limit creation of money for fear that people would stop using the currency and reduce their seigniorage. The volatility of the economy would be reduced, helping everyone, especially the poor.

With no bank regulation, banks might allow their big depositors to audit the bank's books to make sure it's not taking excessive risks.

A Note about the Stock Market

With government backing off, the economy would become less volatile. But the stock market would not, because the price/earnings ratios would be higher[8]. When the price/earnings ratio of the market is 20, minor economic fluctuations (without government intrusions) might cause minor fluctuations in stock prices. But if the PE ratio of the market were 80, minor economic fluctuations would cause significant fluctuations of prices. The stock market never feels safe. For short-term investors, it must never *be* safe. If it were, people would sell everything they've got, borrow up to the hilt, throw it all into the stock market, and come out millionaires. Price/earnings ratios are always high enough to prevent this unrealistic scenario.

---

8. If a company's earnings are $1.00 a share and the price of the stock is $25, the price/earnings ratio (PE) would be 25. If a company has no earnings, the PE ratio is infinite.

PRIVATIZE THE MONETARY SYSTEM

April 8, 2019. Whoever creates money earns profit. It's called seigniorage. The U.S. Treasury spends less than twenty cents to mint a hundred dollar bill. It sells the bill for a hundred bucks, which isn't a bad way to make living. Not only that, most of our money consists of electronic bank deposits, which cost nothing to create. Governments love that seigniorage.

American government has done a lousy job of managing its monetary system. Let's consider delegating the job to the people. To do this, the government would have to give up its monopoly over the dollar. Anything could serve as legal tender. All currencies would be convertible into every other, enabling people to select those that are most convenient and which best hold their values.[9]

Competition provides a natural barrier against a currency's overproduction. If one producer goes hog-wild about earning seigniorage and creates an excess of money, the prices of products valued in that currency would rise. Consumers would therefore stop using that currency, and the producer's seigniorage would come to a halt. Currency producers would have to balance short-term against long-term goals, making the system self-regulating. Regulation apart from government is good.

The advantage of a multi-currency system: The government would no longer control the monetary system. That's a big deal. The government could continue to produce dollars, but dollars would count as only one currency among many.

The disadvantage of the multi-currency system: Having more than

---

9. For you cognoscenti, this is called Thiers' Law, the opposite of Gresham's Law. Gresham's Law applies when there are two currencies, but the government fixes the price between them, as prevailed with gold and silver in the U.S. in the 19th Century. Under those circumstances, the bad currency (silver) drove out the good currency (gold, which disappeared, mostly overseas). Under Thiers' Law, the price between the currencies is not set by the government. It's set by a free market, constantly fluctuating. Under those circumstances, the good currency drives out the bad. Even if there are three or more currencies, Thiers' Law still applies as long as each currency can be freely exchanged with each of the others.

one currency would be cumbersome. But not impossible. The Europeans accommodated many currencies for years.

No matter what system is used, most long-term lenders should require that the repayment of loans be made in a currency whose value is tied to gold.

Both the multi-currency system and the gold standard would reduce inflation and make the value of money relatively level. Either approach would be a tremendous improvement over America's current, free-wheeling monetary management. The multi-currency approach would have the further advantage of excluding government altogether from the management of the monetary system.

THE OVERREACHING FEDERAL RESERVE

August 15, 2020. While rioters have weakened America at the periphery, the Federal Reserve weakens it from its very heart.

The most important prices in the entire economy are the prices of U.S. Treasury bonds, especially long-term bonds. What makes them so special?

Companies make long-term commitments when they plan new fac-tories and the facilities needed to generate future sales. To pay for them, they sell long-term bonds and repay the bonds from those far-off earn-ings. In deciding whether to build the facilities, companies balance the interest rates they must pay on the bonds against expected future sales and profits.

The Federal Reserve Bank now plans to force the interest rates on U.S. Treasuries down, indirectly lowering the rates on corporate bonds as well.

When the Fed sets the cost of long-term borrowing too low, com-panies overborrow and overbuild those long-term facilities, creating an imbalance that's likely to cause an economic downturn. The know-it-all

Federal Reserve Bank, having caused numerous economic downturns in the past, is laying the groundwork for another.

Article I, Section 8 of the U.S. Constitution gives Congress the power to "coin money, regulate the value thereof and of foreign coin." The Tenth Amendment provides that "The powers not delegated to the United States by the Constitution...are reserved to the States respectively or to the people."

A literal reading of the Constitution – the way the courts *should* read it – would prevent the Federal Reserve from setting interest rates because the Constitution does not authorize it.

I know, liberals want a "living" Constitution, interpreted as judges see fit under current circumstances. But if liberals continue to increase the size and intrusiveness of government, American civilization will die a painful death, with the poor hurt most.

The Federal Reserve Bank has been asked to:

- Prevent inflation

- Create full employment

- Prevent financial crises

- Shrink the trade deficit

- Tackle climate change, and

- Eliminate racial economic disparities.

Lots of luck, Fed. Except for preventing inflation, no central bank can do any of those things.

But the Fed isn't even trying to prevent inflation. It's striving for 2% inflation and has expressed disappointment that the rate has prevailingly been lower. Forget it. The right policy is no inflation at all.

Congress and the Fed have caused severe economic downturns. They should quit trying.

It's bad enough that the Fed has spent a decade buying longer-term government securities and mortgage-backed securities. Now, the Fed is loaning money directly to U.S. corporations, large and small. The Fed governors will have crony capitalist friends emerging from the bushes to get in on the action.

Even more unconstitutional, the Fed is thinking about keeping the interest rates low on all maturities of Treasury securities. Good grief! The economic distortions would eventually become monumental.

The Fed intends to use its powers during the pandemic until the economy is "solidly on the road to recovery." How will they know? By the time an economic trend becomes apparent, it's too late for a government reaction.

Besides, too much of the money being handed out by the government to stimulate the economy sits in personal and corporate bank accounts, stimulating nothing until governors open the state economies.

The Fed has increased its cash on hand from $1 trillion to $4 trillion. (The Fed simply writes numbers in its own bank accounts. Handy, huh?) Will these stupendous cash reserves, equal to Germany's annual economy, eventually cause inflation significantly higher than 2%? The Federal Reserve governors don't think so, but I think they'll be wrong again.

Central economic planning is not only unconstitutional, it makes the economy more volatile, causing severe downturns that are especially hard on the poor. The Fed should be abolished and the entire federal government should stop trying to improve the economy. In the long run, central planning cannot help but fail.

Chapter 3 – Details Concerning the Thirty-Seven Hurts

Government Lotteries Breed Poverty

September 18, 2017. Government lotteries trigger gambling addictions and breed poverty. Is this what you want your state government to be doing?

States advertise lotteries aggressively in poor areas. New York says, "Hey, you never know." California says, "Imagine what a buck could do!" Slogans like these encourage people to treat lotteries as investments, not entertainment. To provide the funds, low-income folks cut necessities.

The chances of winning a recent $759 million jackpot were 1-in-292 million. Not exactly a sure bet. On average, one dollar spent on lottery tickets returns a lousy 52 cents – worse than the returns of private gambling companies.

State governments rake in nearly $70 billion a year from lotteries, supposedly for education. Baloney! Education is what the legislators *say* they're spending the lottery money on, because it sounds good. But money is fungible and has no strings attached; it can go wherever the legislators please from day to day.

Legislators love lotteries because they raise revenues, but also enable the legislators to avoid being blamed for raising taxes for education.

Lotteries are taxes, regressive taxes, taking more money from the poor than from the rich.

Governments spend billions on nutrition and housing programs. Lotteries encourage the poor to cut those same necessities. Let's get rid of these abominable taxes on the poor.

Occupational Licensing Hurts the Poor Big Time[10]

June 6, 2018. Almost a third of Americans need government permission to do their jobs. Occupational licenses require fees and long periods of training that low-income people can't afford.

People already in a business lobby government to keep others out. The shortage of workers results in higher prices for their products. The poor get hit twice: They're excluded from the jobs, and they pay higher prices for their purchases.

An Institute for Justice's occupational licensing report looked at 102 low-to-moderate-income occupations in all 50 states and the District of Columbia.[11] It found that, on average, licenses cost $209 in fees, require nine months of training, and the passing of a state-approved examination. Pretty stiff requirements for people who need jobs to get by.

Every state licenses hair stylists, requiring an average of 372 days of training. A black woman wants to make a living braiding hair? Fine. Just fork over for a year of unnecessary training.

You want to shine shoes on the streets of Washington, DC? That'll be $1,500 in fees, please.

10. Mercatus Center, Matthew D. Mitchell, *Occupational Licensing and the Poor and Disadvantaged,* 8/28/17.
AIER, Paz Gomez, *Lift the Occupational Licensing Blockage on Louisiana,* 3/23/18.
WSJ, *A Model for Licensing Reform,* 4/4/18.
WSJ, Shoshana Weissman & C. Jarrett Dieterle, *Is It Wrong to Cut a Homeless Man's Hair Without a License?* (I didn't record the date.)
11. AIER, Veronique de Rugy, *Want to be an Eyelash Technician? You Will Need a License for That,* 1/7/19.

Mayor Bloomberg banned salty or fatty food donations to NYC home-less. Going hungry beats consuming salt and fat, right?

Many states impose onerous requirements on child day-care centers. Mothers who can't pay the high costs must stay home to take care of the kids and cannot obtain employment outside.

Requirements that mandate college degrees exclude many minorities.

Louisiana licenses florists. Yes, it's so important for government to protect citizens from unattractive flower arrangements.

Ex-cons don't have the money for training and fees. Doesn't matter; they can always return to crime.

The purpose of licensing boards is to protect the turf of those already in the business and to raise money for the state. Consumers, not govern-ment boards, should choose those who serve them by buying from some and not from others. Free markets help everyone except bureaucrats. Freedom from government interference helps the poor most.

Rent Control

February 12, 2018. With rents rising, lawmakers in several states want to impose rent control. Eventually, this will make life harder for the very people the policy is intended to help. Here's why: For as long as a tenant remains in an apartment, rent control requires the landlord to keep the rent level, even if the tenant remains for years, paying amounts too low to cover the landlord's rising costs. Who is this likely to benefit?

Older, prosperous people who seldom move because their lives are stable.

When tenants move out, the landlord can lift the rent to market rates for the new tenants. Who is likely to pay the higher rates?

Younger and less prosperous people whose lives are less stable and who move frequently.

In place of rent control, government should keep the rents at market rates and encourage builders to construct more apartments.

But why haven't the builders already constructed more apartments?

Because of building restrictions.

Well then, government could help the poor by removing the restrictions.

Ah, but most building restrictions were imposed because voters who are relatively prosperous and whose lives are stable demanded them.

All too true. If legislators were limited to only one term each, they could disregard such political pressure. Non-professional politicians might even serve as leaders and teach their constituents about the dynamics of rent control. Small government fosters communities of caring. Big government, quite the opposite.

RACIST MINIMUM WAGES

January 16, 2017. At the beginning of 2017, some twenty states raised their minimum wages. This not only hurt the poor, it was racist. The right level of minimum wage is zero.

The hourly labor of some poorly educated blacks in U.S. central cities, especially young black males, is worth less than the minimum wage. It is not racist for an employer to refuse to hire such persons. It is the minimum wage laws themselves that are racist. They prevent people, especially poor blacks, from being employed.

As black economist Thomas Sowell put it, "The real minimum wage is zero. This is what inexperienced and low-skilled people receive because of legislation making it illegal for employers to pay them what they're worth."

A young person who is not hired doesn't learn to show up for work on time and to accept supervision. He doesn't step on the first rung of the ladder of success.

The employment rate of young black American males is upward of

50%. This anecdotal percentage applies to economic conditions prevailing before President Trump's reduction of tax rates and significant cancellation of regulations, after which unemployment rates reached historic lows for both black and Hispanic workers. As economist Milton Friedman said, "Minimum wages are the most racist laws on the books."

Workers not subject to minimum wages include newspaper delivery workers, seasonal farm workers, and telephone switchboard operators. Also, millions of small businesses with annual revenues below $500,000 that do not engage in interstate commerce are exempt from minimum wage laws. The total number of workers paid less than minimum wages outnumber those subject to the minimum by almost three times. Every time the minimum wage has been increased, the number of people who lose their minimum wage jobs and find jobs at below minimum wage is significantly greater than the number who remain at the minimum wage.[12] Minimum wage increases also force some employees to change from full-time to part-time work.

Liberals note that even the minimum wages imposed by government do not supply employees with an adequate standard of living. This is all too true. But I count 37 ways, not including minimum wages, that U.S. governments make life harder and more expensive for the poor. If the governments stopped doing those things, almost everyone would benefit, and those now earning the lowest incomes would then earn far more than the current minimum wage.

What would people from the public sector do after they've been let go? They could do something helpful to society for a change.

The average person subject to minimum wage has a household income of $53,000, many being the wives of working husbands or young people living at home. Few people earn their livelihood solely from minimum wage.

---

12. AIER, Alan Reynolds, *When the Minimum Wage Rises, a Million More Fall Below Minimum,* 8/26/20.

Minimum wage laws provide little good, but they do substantial harm. They should all be repealed.

UNIONS HURT THE POOR AND REDUCE CARING

January 1, 2018. American unions are rich, powerful, and independent fiefdoms. They couldn't exist in their present form without federal labor laws to support them. Those laws should be repealed. The government should have nothing to do with the interactions between employers and employees.

Government's involvement in labor issues makes the wages of union members unnaturally high. This raises costs for everyone else. The poor, who spend a larger portion of their income on living expenses, are hurt the most.

Unions prevent poor teachers in central city schools from being fired because the unions want those union dues to continue rolling in. Quality education for blacks? Naah, who cares about that?

Government's involvement puts employers on the defensive and increases hostility all around.

The more that government forcibly intercedes on behalf of employees, the less employers care about the employees themselves. More government means less caring.

Without unions, many employers would increasingly reveal to their employees as much as possible about the company's finances. Many employers would collaborate increasingly with employees, exploring how they can best work together. Less government means more caring.

Without government intercession, employees could form unions as a means of expressing their needs to the employer. And, of course, employees could choose to leave a job and find another.

Current pension laws tend to prevent employees from leaving their jobs. All pension laws should be repealed. They are none of government's business. If employees want a pension plan, they and their employer can set up whatever suits them. Without government involvement, employees would gain increasing knowledge of investment matters.

Major beneficiaries of government-supported unions are union leaders, who are paid substantial salaries. Also, members of the U.S. Congress, especially the Democratic members, like the substantial campaign gifts they receive from unions.

GEORGE FLOYD WAS KILLED BY A UNION, NOT RACISM

Derek Chauvin, the policeman who killed George Floyd, has been the subject of more than a dozen complaints and has been given several letters of reprimand for the excessive use of force. The three other cops who stood by and watched Floyd's murder have been disciplined for the same reason. Why haven't they all been fired?

Because of the Minneapolis Police Union.

An article in the June 6 issue of the Wall Street Journal reveals that the Minneapolis Police Union has successfully prevented all four of the officers from being fired in the past. Even now, after the death of George Floyd, the union is gearing up with defense attorneys to save their jobs.

The chief of police of the Minneapolis Police Department is black. You don't think the entire department is racist, do you? Come on! Assign blame where it belongs: the union.

Any member of Congress who accepts campaign contributions from unions and acts to protect them should be relieved of duty. Better yet, the wretched federal laws that give unions their power should be repealed.

REDUCE POLICE FUNDING [13]

June 13, 2019. Do you want to cut back police departments? Fine, providing the community meets the following conditions:

- Any member of the public can carry weapons, hidden or not, without a license. To some extent, the public would police itself. Not until the 1880s, a hundred years after American independence, did police departments operate in all major U.S. cities. But the public was not troubled by criminal activity during that time. The pressure to create police departments developed mostly because businesses couldn't or wouldn't obtain proper insurance for their property losses or liabilities. They preferred to lay the cost onto the public.

- Police departments may not unionize. Bad cops can be fired.

- People can run for election to serve as policemen in the communities where they live.

- All victimless crimes are repealed. The criminalization of drugs is out. Prostitution is in.

- Insurance companies can raise premiums immediately on drivers who speed or commit driving violations. Speeding is enforced by onboard monitoring devices, and intersection cams are operated by a consortium of insurers. Insurance companies would work with police as to the reasonableness of violations. If speed limits and other laws are too stringent, too many violations would ensue. If they're too lenient, violations would be too few.

- Businesses cannot obtain financing unless they have proper insurance against physical loss, theft, and liability. Insurance companies would coordinate with banks and finance companies to agree on the proper conditions.

---

13. AIER Robert E. Wright, *History Reveals the Alternative to the Police State,* 6/10/20.

NATIONAL PSYCHOSIS

From 1776 to the 1830s, America had no police departments. It was only in the 1880s that all major cities had them. Until then, armed citizens did their own policing.

You might respond that we can't arm everybody in the present day. There's too much psychosis.

You have a point. After a friend obtained a degree in social work, she started giving psychiatric therapy in a poor area of New Jersey. She couldn't handle it; the people had too many problems.

Of course they did. Poor areas are where the federal government tries hardest to be helpful. The long-term, actual results of most government policies are opposite to the intended results. The consequence is psychosis and unhappiness. The greater the presence of force in a society, the more psychosis that results. Government should back off and let people work things out themselves. (Government workers are not about to back off on their own. They have to be forced to do so by voters.)

Anyway, the people would work it out far more quickly than one would think. It is only when government gets involved, by retaining large government police departments with powerful unions, for example, that the results are laborious, expensive and in the long run, failures.

CRIMINALIZATION OF DRUGS: A DISASTER

In 1925, H.L. Mencken wrote, "Prohibition has not only failed in its promises but created additional serious and disturbing social problems throughout society. There is not less drunkenness in the Republic, but more. There is not less crime, but more. The cost of government is not smaller, but vastly greater. Respect for the law has not increased, but diminished."

The War on Drugs, which is international, has been far more damaging than was the prohibition of alcohol in the 1920s. Alcohol's prohibition lasted for thirteen years. Drug's prohibition has lasted for half a century. Both wars were lost from the very beginning.

When a product is criminalized, the price rises. This attracts people who are willing to risk disobeying the law. They, in turn, increase the supply.

When drugs appear on the street that weren't there before, people are intrigued and buy them. If the drugs are addictive, the users get hooked. Normally, higher demand increases the supply. But with illegal products, it's the other way around: A bigger supply increases the demand.

People who supply illegal drugs would be jailed if they went to court to defend their property rights against other suppliers. Instead, they defend their rights with violence or the threat of violence, mostly on the streets and homes where low-income people live. The drug laws are America's biggest source of violence.

Latin America has only 8% of the world's population. But, mostly because of America's drug laws, Latin American nations have one-third of the world's homicides.[14] Much of El Salvador is ruled by transnational criminal networks that terrorize the population. Some people in the caravan now approaching America are families trying to get away from the violence.[15]

Drug laws have created the Mexican cartels and significantly increased the corruption of law enforcement and elected officials.

America's attempt to eradicate the cultivation of opium in Afghanistan has empowered and funded the Taliban. This has greatly helped America's foreign policy, of course. As Senator Claghorn, a satirical character on the Fred Allen radio show, used to say, "That was a joke, son."

When government enforcement interdicts the transportation of

---

14. WSJ, Rachel Kleinfeld, *The Violence Driving Migration Isn't Just Gangs,* 11/11/18.
15. WSJ, Mary Anastasia O'Grady, *The Drug War and the Caravan,* 11/11/18.

drugs, suppliers respond by making the drugs more powerful. This increases the profits on the drugs that get through. More powerful drugs: Yes, that's great for the nation's health.

America's cost of the drug war has exceeded $1 trillion. More than 1.5 million people have been arrested, disproportionately blacks and Hispanics. How many potential black entrepreneurs, instead of starting businesses, have instead ended up stewing in jail? Drug laws hurt everyone, but they hurt the poor most of all.

The money used in the war on drugs has been unavailable for programs that could reduce overdoses and infectious diseases. Shouldn't drugs be treated as a medical problem and not a criminal problem? Naah, that's too much to ask.

Half a million Americans are incarcerated because they've possessed drugs or sold them peacefully to those who chose to buy them.

The war is fought among the poor. Many potential black entrepreneurs end up tragically as convicted felons, a black mark for life. If children of the elite were being jailed in significant numbers, the war on drugs would quickly be terminated.

When the cops make a drug arrest, they send the money to the federal government, which returns 80% of it to the police department from which the arrest was made. The department uses it to acquire things it needs. But the police would never abuse their conflict of interest, of course.

No, the war on drugs is similar to the prohibition of alcohol in the 1920s. In every respect, it has done enormous harm.

BORDER RESTRICTIONS MAKE DRUG PROBLEMS WORSE[16]

December 31, 2018. President Trump has claimed that building a border wall would pay for itself by limiting illicit drugs entering the country.

A border wall may reduce illegal immigration, Mr. President, but it will make the drug problem worse.

Border restrictions increase the cost of transporting drugs. Drug demand, however, remains the same. Dealers, therefore, increase drug concentrations, making overdosing more likely and hurting the poor most. Nothing new there. After restrictions were imposed on regular cocaine, dealers developed the devastating crack cocaine.

Higher transportation barriers also cause smaller drug dealers to drop out of the market, leaving the better connected and more violent dealers in charge. This occurred during Prohibition in the 1920s, when Al Capone and other big-time gangsters took over.

When any product that people want to buy is made illegal, they buy it anyway. The illegality may even stimulate additional buying. People are funny that way.

Liberals like drug laws because they get their kicks out of imposing force. Conservatives may support the laws in part because of religious impulses which, in the 19th Century, induced people to avoid playing cards on Sundays.

Those who supply the product cannot go to court to defend their property rights as dealers. They defend their rights with violence or the threat of violence. The prohibition of drugs accordingly is an important source of violence in America and the world. The criminalization of any product or service that people want to purchase always fosters a violent underworld that seeks high profits for disobeying the law.

The prohibition of alcohol failed for more than ten years. The pro-

---

16. AIER. Don Lim, *A Border Wall Will Worsen the Drug Problem,* 12/11/18.

hibition of drugs has failed for 50 years (at a monstrous $41 billion a year). The only realistic solutions: decriminalization, and education about drugs. Let's dip our toes into those alternatives. They will reduce addictions and save a bundle.

CIVIL ASSET FORFEITURES[17]

Civil asset forfeitures exemplify government overreach.

A group of people are driving on an interstate in a car that has an out-of-state license plate. The police stop them because a car wheel touched the line at the edge of the road. Explanation by the passengers about where they're going doesn't hold together. The police search the car and find a large amount of cash, which is assumed to be drug-related. The police send the cash to the federal government. Under the "Equitable Sharing Program," the local cops get back 80% of the money, which is used to benefit the department. The occupants of the car are not entitled to free legal help. The seizure is generally not contested because the cost of legal counsel to defend the rights of the accused is greater than the value of the property taken.

(Police are aware that cars of this nature going out of a city are likely to hold cash. Cars going toward a city are more likely to carry drugs.)

Some years ago in Detroit, the police seized one hundred cars of patrons of an art institute because the institute had failed to obtain a liquor license.

Did somebody say overreach?

If your property is taken, you must prove your innocence. If you don't succeed within a certain time, the property is taken for good.

In New Mexico and Nebraska, assets can be forfeited only after the

---

17. Heritage Foundation, *The Police Can Take Your Stuff: The Civil Forfeiture Reforms We Still Need*, 8/22/19.
AIER, Stephen C. Miller, *Civil Asset Forfeiture Undermines Free Enterprise and Human Dignity*, 1/27/18.

owner has been convicted, not just arrested. But in the other 48 states, as the law puts it, the cops need only convict the property. Very convenient; property doesn't talk back.

From 2000 to 2020, some $36 billion was taken as civil asset forfeitures. In 2014, the amounts exceeded those of burglaries. In most states, civil asset forfeitures are profit centers for law enforcement.

They also eradicate civil rights. For police departments to gain financial benefits from such arrests is outrageous.

U.S. OBESITY CAUSED BY FEDERAL SUBSIDIES[18]

August 13, 2018. The U.S. Farm Bill of 1973 assured consumers a plentiful supply of food at reasonable prices. Under the bill and its successors, some $20 billion is paid annually to rich farmers who produce staple commodities, especially corn.

Foods produced from these crops – French fries, pastas, pizzas, breads, condiments, sweet deserts, sweet drinks, and especially high-fructose corn syrup – are unhealthy. These also being the cheapest, the people hurt most are the poor.

Around the same year, 1973, American obesity began to increase. More than 40% of Americans can now be classified as obese. Mississippi and West Virginia rank high in obesity.[19]

Beginning in 2016, American life expectancy began to fall. Mississippi ranks 47th in life expectancy and West Virginia 51st.[20] Mississippi has been hit especially hard by COVID-19.

Members of the 1973 Congress were just trying to be helpful to a few thousand farmers. Little did they realize that, decades later, millions of Americans would be obese, a disastrous public health condition.

---

18. AIER. Jeffrey A. Tucker, *Why Unhealthy Food is Cheap and Plentiful,* 5/21/18.
19. Robert Wood Johnson Foundation, *Adult Obesity Rates,* September 2019.
20. Reuters, Hilary Brueck and Jenny Cheng, *These are the US states where people live the longest, healthiest lives – and the shortest.* 4/16/18.

America is going soft because government made it so. The best way the government can become more helpful is to stop being helpful.

If the subsidies to rich farmers were terminated, as they should be, the supply of bad foods would fall, and their prices would rise. But people still have to eat. The demand for good foods would therefore increase. Suppliers of good foods would compete to meet the demand. With the creativity of free market capitalism, the supply would eventually overwhelm the demand, and the prices of good foods would fall.

Did you get that? It's common sense economics, which liberals make every effort not to understand.

CRONY CAPITALISM

December 31, 2016. Society works best, especially for the poor, when the powers of government are limited. Big companies and crony capitalism make this difficult to achieve. Here's an illustration:

A carpenter named Scott has three employees, several thousand dollars of tools, a truck, and a mobile phone. His business is successful, and his wife homeschools the children. He can say to the federal government, "I don't need you. I want you out of my life, with low tax rates and few regulations."

Alternatively, consider a hypothetical company with more than 50,000 employees that builds solar panels and wind farms. It's pretty much controlled by the CEO, named George. The company pays more than a million dollars to Washington lobbyists. George instructs them, "Tell the administration and members of Congress we're willing to invest plenty of money in renewable sources of energy, such as wind farms. But since renewables are less efficient than the energy produced by fossil fuels, we want the government to give us tax advantages that will encourage renewable production. Our business is large enough to deal with federal regulations. We want the feds to impose plenty of them to hinder upstart companies from competing with us, even though they may be more efficient than we are." (That latter part George mumbles under his breath.)

Scott controls his own company and wants government to be limited. George's company, and many others, want government's help. That's called crony capitalism.

Corporations are not wrong to seek government's help. It's their job to maximize earnings for the shareholders. If government officials are willing to be bribed by campaign gifts, the companies should take advantage. But it is woefully wrong of government officials to accept such gifts and grant such help.

The reason why America got started as a democracy is because, for the first time in world history, most citizens owned their own land and their own businesses. (At the beginning, most businesses were farms.) Like Scott, they generally didn't need government and didn't want its interference. They developed a constitution that endeavored to limit the power of the federal government by diversifying it among the executive, the legislature, and the courts. The constitution provided that all powers not specifically granted to the federal government were reserved to the states or to the people.

Democracy these days is more difficult to sustain. Unlike Scott, most people do not own their own businesses. Many are employees. Some are on welfare. Almost 20% are employees of gargantuan federal, state, and local governments. Many work for large companies that are controlled by relatively few people. These companies often want government's help, and they find government officials who, unfortunately, are willing to provide it.

Society works best when the means of production are widely owned and when government is small and unobtrusive. One solution comes at election time, when voters can remove from office those legislators who fail to keep government limited.

An excellent solution is to do away with all kinds of federal welfare, including Social Security, Medicare, and all crony capital assistance to businesses. To the greatest possible extent, people should supply their own needs. When they can't, with income tax rates significantly lowered, private individuals or associations would raise funds from the prosperous and provide it to those who display obvious need. They would employ social workers to help them get on their own two feet.

THE WAR ON POVERTY CREATES DEPENDENCY[21]

November 5, 2018. The War on Poverty was first funded in 1966. During the twenty years prior, the poverty rate of households in the lowest one-fifth of earned income improved markedly, falling from 32% to 15%. (The poverty rate is the percentage of people the government claims to live in poverty.) But in the half-century since 1966, despite the War on Poverty, the poverty rate, still based on the earned income of the lowest fifth, hasn't budged.

Look at that one more time: For twenty years prior to passage of the War on Poverty, the poverty rate improved markedly. In the fifty years since, the poverty rate has stayed about the same.

But, of course, say government aficionados, this happened for other reasons.

What reasons?

We'll know more about that after we pass legislation to repair it.

Back to the War on Poverty. Since the war started in 1966, the poverty rate based on the earned income of the lowest fifth has not changed. But the *total* income of that lowest sector has soared. Counting food stamps, Medicaid, children's health insurance, the refunded portion of earned-income tax credits, and more than 85 other means-tested federal and state benefits, the poverty rate of the lowest income level would be 3%,

21. WSJ, Phil Gramm and John F. Early, *Government Can't Rescue the Poor,* 10/10/18.

not 15%. The rate would fall even further if transfers within families, non-governmental charity, and unreported income were counted.

The bureaucrats don't publish this because the last thing they want is to make their jobs unnecessary.

Government transfer payments have essentially eliminated American poverty. For the lowest fifth of U.S. households, more than 84% of their disposable income comes from government transfer payments.

But the purpose of the War on Poverty was not just to raise living standards, it was also to make the poor self-sufficient. On this account, the effort has failed. In 2015, the lowest fifth of earned income, compared with the middle fifth, had 37% more families whose head was of prime working age but no one in the family was working.

The War on Poverty should be repealed, and the government should stop collecting statistics. All charity should be left to non-governmental agencies and private citizens. They would not only provide needed funds, they would also induce people to take jobs.

Government Welfare

Government welfare creates dependency. Say a woman who receives $200 a week from welfare is offered $300 a week from a 40-hour-a-week job. But the job would terminate her welfare, making her effective income rise by only $100 a week. That comes to $2.50 an hour. Wisely, she chooses to remain on welfare.

Private welfare organizations would deal with this issue with greater flexibility, making sure that welfare recipients obtain jobs whenever possible.

Government welfare also creates emotional dependency and low self-image. One might say to a welfare recipient, "Why not go out and get a job?"

"I couldn't do that. I'm better off where I am, watching television all day."

THE GREAT SOCIETY[22]

Lyndon B. Johnson's Great Society programs have been in place for 55 years. Many *trillions* of dollars have been spent on Medicaid, food stamps, welfare, public housing, rent subsidies, and federal aid to public schools.

The results have been wonderful, haven't they? Neighborhoods in city centers, all under the control of "progressive" Democrats, are as poor, crime-ridden, under-educated, and unhealthy as they were when LBJ promised those big changes, if not worse.

That so-called Great Society has been a miserable and extraordinarily expensive failure. Let's chuck it before America goes over the cliff.

SOCIALISM

My friend Barb said she's basically a socialist.

Barb, I didn't realize you favor violence. A socialist government would enact even more laws and regulations than we already have. You'd be disobeying one or more of the rules within about three minutes. The state would then have the right to come down on you with violence to your person or property.

The bigger the government, the more rich people ponder ways to ensure the election of their friends so the rich can benefit all the more from crony capitalism.

Funny. Laws that are designed to help the poor have counterintuitive effects that, in the long run, hurt the poor. But the laws designed to help the rich work dead on every time with no problem.

The more violence enacted by government to enforce its laws and regulations, the more violence permeates society in general, such as rioting in the streets. But, of course, we can reduce all that by enacting gun laws and doing away with the Second Amendment.

---

22. WSJ, Daniel Henninger, *America's New Nihilism,* 6/4/20.

Barb, if the total tax burden on your income were only, say, 7%, wouldn't you reach out to those in your community who need help? Or at least help fund others who make a living assisting the needy? Of course you would, and so would millions of others.

Besides, needy people would be fewer in number. In a free market society with very low tax rates, government would not be making life more difficult and more expensive for them in the 38 ways described in this book.

The imposing Capital Building in Washington implies that we should look up to members of Congress since it's assumed they're usually right. But until the members reduce the size and intrusiveness of government, it would be more appropriate for them to meet in Quonset huts, since they're usually wrong.

HOUSING FOR THE POOR

Here are the best ways to make available housing for the poor:

- Do away with federal housing subsidies, and

- Do away with zoning laws, regulations, and rent control laws, which limit the building of housing.

The private sector would then produce multi-family housing projects in greater abundance, with better quality and attractiveness, than prevails now in current subsidized government housing projects.

While we're at it, let's close down Housing Urban Development (HUD), a Cabinet member, to save $40 billion in federal costs and enable its 8,000 employees to do something useful.

ANTI-PROSTITUTION

It is outrageous for a prominent elderly widower to be arrested for seeing a prostitute. The customers aren't responsible for mistreating the employees or holding them against their will. Mistreatment of that kind occurs because government makes prostitution illegal. The illegality attracts thugs who seek high profits because they're willing to disobey the law. Those are the people who mistreat women.

Some low-income women need prostitution to support themselves, but without being considered criminals, thank you. In legal industries, severe mistreatment of employees is rare. Holding people against their will is even more rare.

Once legalized, prostitutes could hold their heads high for performing a valuable service.

CHILD CARE

Government regulations can make child care unobtainable for people who most need it – those of low income.

For example, child care for Massachusetts toddlers[23] averages $18,845, or 65% of the state's average single parent's income. In Mississippi, the cost is $4,670, less than 25% of a single parent's income.

It's true that the overall cost of living in Massachusetts is half again higher than that of Mississippi. But this doesn't explain the huge disparity in child care costs. That disparity is because the child care regulations in Massachusetts are far more onerous than those of Mississippi. The high user costs makes it nearly impossible for low-income citizens of Massachusetts to obtain child care.

With both prostitution and child care, government makes life harder for the poor.

23. AIER, Max Gulker, *Why Does Child Care in Massachusetts Cost Four Times What it Does in Mississippi?* 2/28/19.

Well, that's what government is supposed to do, right?

PRICE CONTROLS ON INTEREST RATES

In recent years, the Federal Reserve Bank has kept interest rates unnaturally low. This has not only deprived savers of reasonable returns, it has also widened the gap between rich and poor. With interest rates low, banks are nevertheless willing to lend to the rich, because the risk is low. But with the interest rates low, banks are reluctant to lend to small businesses and common folks because of the higher risks.

Gosh, says the Fed, we didn't think about that.

REAL ESTATE MARKETS COULD ENRICH THE POOR

March 12, 2018. If government would get out of the way, housing markets could enrich the poor.[24]

Here's how automobile markets enrich the poor. New cars cost more than they're worth. Used cars cost less than they're worth. As cars move down the income ladder, sales by the rich and purchases by the poor transfer billions of dollars of value from rich to poor.

This happens naturally; no one set it up. Here is what makes this possible: Government interferes relatively little with automobile markets.

Given a chance, real estate markets could do the same. Prosperous people would overpay to build houses. When they vacate, the less prosperous would underpay to move in. Billions of dollars of value would transfer from rich to poor.

Government prevents this, partly because it owns 28% of the entire nation, including 85% of Nevada and more than half each of Utah, Alaska, and Oregon. Surely, at least some of this immensity of land could be made available for sale!

---

24. I don't believe I invented this idea, but once it was planted in my mind, I could certainly run with it. The percentages of federal ownership of states are available on the Web.

Indian tribes, isolated in reserves, live in misery on land equivalent to the State of Idaho. They would be better off if they were integrated with the rest of society, as they should have been from the beginning.

Zoning thwarts real estate sales. Houston, Texas, gets along fine without zoning. Chemical plants are not built in residential areas. Residential land is too expensive.

Land use laws, building laws, banking laws, environmental, farming, mining, water, tax, and who knows what other laws all interfere with real estate sales. Most of those social and economic needs could be satisfied better by the private sector, backed by the courts.

Everywhere it turns, government unintentionally hurts the disadvantaged.

RAMPAGE BY ROTTEN EGGS

September 7, 2020. The Wall Street Journal nailed it: The attorneys general of New York, West Virginia, and Texas have laid a rotten egg. They're suing Ohio's Hillandale Farms for price gouging on the sale of eggs.

Americans had become accustomed to spending almost half their food dollars on meals outside the home. Suddenly, the lockdowns forced them to prepare three squares a day in their own kitchens. The demand for eggs soared.

Caught short, the egg producers had to withhold a portion of the eggs they'd intended to sell and leave them under lamps to hatch chicks, which matured into laying hens. This took several weeks, a stunningly short time.

Nationwide, the price quadrupled. In New York, West Virginia, and Texas, egg prices did a little better – they only tripled.

Without some monetary incentive, egg suppliers could have serviced only their largest customers. Smaller stores, including those in low-income neighborhoods, would probably have received none.

Adjusting prices upward enables shortages to end as soon as possible. If shortages are especially intense in New York, higher prices draw products from where modest surpluses prevail. Gouging laws cause shortages to persist, especially among people with low income.

Enlightened states have no anti-gouging laws. The three anti-gouging attorneys general should be targets of egg-throwing contests.

SOCIAL SECURITY INEQUITY

June 6, 2020. Social Security benefits terminate when a person dies. The life expectancy of black men is significantly shorter than the life expectancy of white women. Therefore, the FICA taxes paid by black men help to support the lives of white women, but not the other way around.

It would be more equitable if we got government out of the deal. All of us should have non-government pension arrangements, to which the funds we contribute serve to benefit ourselves. It doesn't take a village, as Hillary Clinton wrote; it takes personal liberty.

GET GOVERNMENT OUT OF HEALTHCARE

Yes, healthcare would be better quality and far less expensive if government had nothing to do with it. Various columns in Chapter 5 explain this in some detail.

TAXING THE RICH DOES NOT HELP THE POOR

September 4, 2017. Say the federal government taxes a rich guy $10,000 and hands out $1,000 to each of ten poor people. This will reduce the gap between rich and poor, right?

Wrong, not in the long run. (The long run is the time scale that government should look at the hardest, but seldom does. Decades of faulty laws and regulations are passed. Almost all of them have hidden and deleterious long-term effects. No one can tell what law or regulation has what effect. The government makes sure to keep its blinders on to avoid seeing anything that might reduce its budgets.)

Okay, back to my story: The feds tax a rich guy ten grand and hands out a thousand to each of ten poor people.

Welfare makes people feel dependent and worthless. Far better that they be employed.

Rich people don't spend all their income. The excess does not lie fallow. It is invested, or it contributes to economic activity in one way or another. If the prosperous are taxed at low rates, they have all the more to contribute to economic activity. Those funds generate jobs for the poor folks. Over the long pull, the jobs raise the income (and morale) of the ten poor folks considerably more than the $1,000 they would otherwise have received in welfare.

Besides, with our gigantic federal government, only a small portion of new revenues actually reaches the poor. Some goes to prosperous crony capitalists, and some pays the salaries of federal bureaucrats, whose average income, including benefits, is way higher than that of average Americans.

About half of American households pay no income taxes. Social Security taxes they pay, but not income taxes. They *should* pay income taxes, however, at the rate of something like 7%, with no deductions or exemptions (and no Social Security tax). That same 7% rate should also apply to the rich, who now pay income taxes at rates of more than 35%.

Intuitively, you'd think that reducing the tax rate of the rich more than that of the poor would benefit the rich more than the poor. But this would be wrong. The actual, long-term results of most government policies are counterintuitive.

For one thing, paying some income taxes would encourage low-income people to become aware of the ridiculous purposes for which the government spends so much and apply pressure on government to knock it off. For another, as just explained, the low tax rate on the rich opens up employment opportunities for the non-rich. In the long run, low income tax rates on everyone, with no deductions or exemptions, would enable the poor to gain wealth faster than the rich.

Legislators should remove their blinders and attend to the people's long-term interests, not the short term.

The Recent Tax Act Will Help Everyone

April 23, 2018. "How are we going to pay for the January tax cut?" asked a friend.

No one needs to pay for it. The act cut the tax *rates*, not revenues. The top rate for individuals was reduced a little, but the top rate for corporations was reduced substantially.

"So what's the big deal about top rates? Don't the bottom rates count too?"

Yes, but not nearly as much. Corporations and wealthy people provide jobs for the rest of us. When their rates are too high, too many of the profits go to the government, making the wealthy unwilling to risk their money to expand their businesses.

When the top tax rates are lowered, the wealthy expand their businesses, hiring folks like you and me. This stimulates the economy, which in turn brings in additional government revenues.

A more active economy helps the poor most. With wages rising, folks at the bottom can forego welfare and find jobs.

Presidents Harding and Coolidge cut the tax rates in the 1920s. The economy and federal revenues both soared.

Presidents Kennedy and Johnson cut the rates in the 1960s. Same result.

President Reagan cut the rates in the 1980s. Again, the economy and revenues soared.

The 2018 tax act and the repeal of damaging regulations, especially EPA regulations, have been of great consequence. Because of them, the House and Senate will likely become Republican in November. I would even hazard a guess, here in April 2018, that the president will also remain Republican in 2021.

TIGHT CONGRESSIONAL TERM LIMITS NEEDED

Members of Congress can remain in office until they're walking zombies. The number of terms they can serve should be sharply limited.

Regardless of party, the longer members of Congress stay in office, the more they vote to expand the power and reach of government, believing increasingly that, unless government does it, it won't be done.

Wrong. Problems are likely to be solved, providing someone outside of government can make a profit.

On hearing the word "profit," big government acolytes picture a rich guy with a vest and good shoes getting richer. Wrong picture. A poor but enterprising woman starts a house-painting business. She's good at it, but she needs a profit to support her family and possibly make the business grow.

Another example: An association of people raises money from the rich and pays it to the poor. Such enterprises would do a better job providing welfare than government, with total costs far less than government's. But they need modest profits to support themselves.

All private enterprises must keep their costs down, lest competition force them out of business. Government is the most expensive way of doing anything, because it has no profits or competition and its employees can't be fired,

We're better off if members of Congress don't hang around long enough to learn the ways of government. Congressmen and senators should be subject to term limits. One term for each sounds about right to me.

In addition, members of Congress should be subject to the same retirement programs and the same laws they impose on everyone else.

Until the pay of members of Congress is reduced big time, as above, here's an interim step: Congressional pay raises should be limited to the lower of the CPI, or 3%, but with no raises at all if the federal government runs a deficit in the previous fiscal year.

REDUCING POLITICAL PROFESSIONALISM

Regardless of party, the longer members of Congress remain in office, the more they favor big government. We've had enough of political professionals who know about government and little else.

How do we reduce political professionalism in the U.S. House and Senate?

By reducing the time they remain in office to one term each and substantially cutting their pay.

We can't cut their pay to zero because this would exclude people who make little money from running for Congress. I suggest that members be paid a salary equal to the mean of the second quintile of income, the group whose earned income runs from 20% to 40% of the nation's earned income.

Legislators should also be paid their legislative and travel expenses, but not housing costs. As the changes recommended in this book are made, the cost of housing in the District of Columbia would fall anyway.

People running for office would not expect to stay. It would be "their turn to serve." They would not stick around long enough to learn the ways of government. They would not expect to go home millionaires, as members often do now. They would repeal, or at least begin to repeal, the millions of laws and regulations that damage the American people.

Limiting legislative terms reduces the pressure to appease interest groups. Legislators could focus on the nation's long-term interests, like big-time cuts in government costs, especially entitlements.

Bill Buckley said he'd rather be governed by the first 2,000 names in the Boston telephone directory than by the 2,000 faculty members of Harvard University. Buckley was dead on.

Where to begin? Start with the areas that cause the most damage. Eliminate the Civil Service System and the Federal Reserve Bank (matters discussed elsewhere in this book).

After the repeals are completed, we would welcome Congress meeting just a few weeks a year.

ZONING DOES GREAT DAMAGE[25]

In major U.S. urban centers, housing is in short supply, resulting in rents rising faster than wages. The cause of the problem is zoning.

The first large-scale zoning ordinance was imposed in Los Angeles in 1908. The purpose was to separate industrial from residential zones. Even this limited objective was unnecessary. Land is expensive in residential areas. Companies prefer to build their factories on inexpensive land. Bingo, the two are separate, except at the margins.

Oh no, that's not sufficient. People wanted perfection even at the margins, and they wanted government to attain it. Government officials were only too delighted to try, because exercising power is their thing.

But voters should understand that human society is not perfectible. Government should be the very last place to try to attain it.

Zoning laws have greatly expanded. Officials now endeavor to set standards of size, dimension, scale, and aesthetic values for buildings and the land surrounding them. They seek to preserve wetlands and desert lands to help the environment, and help the poor as well.

25. AIER, Jose Nino, *Zoning: The Nemesis of Housing Affordability*, 11/7/17.

The ordinances have grown into multi-layered regulatory boon-doggles. City-planning bureaucrats delay and even ban the construction of housing units, reducing the supply of housing, causing rents to rise.

Guess who pays rents? That's right: those with lower income. Zoning laws, therefore, hit the poor hardest. Their wages have not kept up with the rent increases.

When people complain that rents are too high, it doesn't occur to officials to truly solve the problem by getting rid of zoning. Horrors! That would reduce their power! No, they tackle the high rents directly by imposing rent control, which creates a whole new set of problems, as explained elsewhere in this chapter.

Zoning laws also separate the various functions of cities. Stable urban areas develop a jumble of purposes mixed together. This creates social cohesion, and it means that more people are out walking on the streets, thus reducing crime. Guess who are the victims of most crime? You got it: the poor. All this emerges from voluntary human action, not top-down planning.

Houston, Texas, has development codes that address how property can be subdivided. But it has no zoning. Well, we'll take what we can get.

FEDERAL REGULATIONS HAVE RUN AMOK

Federal regulations must be reduced. In President Obama's final year, the Federal Register, containing public notices of all rules and regula-tions, hit a whopping 97,110 pages.

In 2018, Washington bureaucrats issued eleven regulations for every law passed by Congress. The cost, $1.9 trillion, was greater than corpo-rate and personal income tax revenues combined. The estimated annual cost to each U.S. household, on average, was at least $14,600.

The annual cost of compliance with regulations amounts to about $2,500 per person. Regulations block innovation, devote resources to compliance instead of growth, and suppress employment. They're a major reason for the nation's anemic rate of growth during the Obama administration.

Obama put in place 600 major regulations with compliance costs of at least $100 million. (George W. Bush, no regulatory piker, imposed 426 major regulations.) Obama's 600 majors cost at least $743 billion, larger than the economies of Norway and Israel combined.

A few pebbles thrown in a stream have no noticeable effect on the water flow. But a carload of pebbles has great effect. At the beginning of the Trump administration, the U.S. economy suffered from carloads and carloads of regulations. Here are examples:[26]

- When President Obama took over, the U.S. ranked third in the ease of doing business. It has fallen to eighth place.

- Eight years ago, 40 days were needed to obtain a construction permit. Now, it's 81 days.

- In 2008, enforcing a contract in America took 300 days. Today, 420 days. (Enforcing a contract in Greece requires more than four years – one reason for the travails of that benighted nation.)

- A company that has a contract or subcontract with the government must establish a plan that will enable its workforce to include 7% disabled.

- The government bans blanket policies on drug testing (wherein all employees of a company are tested). Why? Because blanket drug testing might be discriminatory. (Liberals have to maintain a favorable self-image, no matter how absurd the policies.)

- Companies are required to adopt the United Nation's system of labeling chemicals. To comply with the relabeling and reclassification requirements, affected companies must spend an estimated $2.1 billion.

26. WSJ. Bret Stephens, *Doomed to Stagnate?* 12/20/16.

- The Dodd-Frank Bill was intended to prevent another financial crisis. It would do no such thing, but the bill is loaded with unnecessary regulations harmful to banking and finance.

- The National Association of Manufacturers estimates that federal regulations have forced manufacturing companies to pay more than $19,500 per employee to remain in compliance with rules and regulations. Who pays the cost? We do, because of the higher prices of the products.

There's hope: For every dollar of new regulatory costs each agency imposes on the private economy, President Trump has ordered that it must relieve the economy of two dollars of burden.

Congress is working on a bill that requires congressional approval before regulations costing $100 million or more would take effect.

An Obamacare rule, up for reversal, requires companies with 50 or more employees to provide healthcare coverage for all of its workers. This has induced companies to limit the number of employees to 49, even though many firms might prefer to expand.

Another administration target: a rule designed to undermine oil and gas fracking on federal land.

Still another: An SEC rule that forces U.S. companies to report payments to foreign governments. The rule would require companies to disclose proprietary information that competitors could use against them.

Congress will repeal a regulation that requires companies to disclose the natural resources they're extracting – a rule that does not apply to foreign companies.

Obama's Stream Protection Rule, already revoked, would have destroyed tens of thousands of mining jobs and put almost two-thirds of the nation's coal reserves off limits.

From 1980 to 2012, the economy grew at the annual rate of 2.7%. In a careful study, the Mercatus Center found that, if federal regulations had been frozen at the 1980 level, the economy would have grown at 3.5% per year instead of 2.7%. The GDP would have been $19.5 trillion instead of $15.2 trillion, about 25% larger. Per capita, Americans would have been $13,000 wealthier.

Even in the starting year of the above Mercatus study, 1980, the Federal Register contained 87,012 pages – only 10,000 fewer than the current number.

Federal regulations are a huge burden. Reductions have begun. Many more are needed.

MORE ON REGULATIONS

When a company is regulated by government, there's a reasonable chance it will comply in a minimal way. Being subject to force makes people act unnaturally; they're inclined to find out what they can get away with.

If the company fails, the managers can say to the government, "We met the requirements of your regulations and failed anyway. We're justified in asking you come to our rescue." Such an argument is especially reasonable if the company is a bank, and it has met the capital requirements imposed by the regulator.

Companies subject to regulation try to make friends with the regulators. After years of friendship, dinners, tickets to sporting events, and gifts of a favorite brand of Scotch, a regulator is unlikely to turn the regulatory screws as tightly as he can.

If government regulation were done away with, some people would expect CEOs to say, "Let's let 'er rip and go for maximum profits!"

For the most part, those expectations would be wrong. When force disappears, most people no longer try to find out what they can get away with. After a time of adjustment, they would try to do what's right. Most companies that go for minimum standards when they're regulated are likely to strive to achieve reasonable, if not excessive, standards when they're not. They would do this for two reasons: One, because they want to. Two, because if misfortunes occur they may be sued. The government's administrative branch may have pulled back, as I wish it would, but the judiciary has not and should not pull back. When someone gets hurt or even feels hurt, the judiciary becomes the regulator. In that respect, force remains, although it's conditional.

Getting sued is a pain in the neck, and it's expensive. Most companies do what they can to avoid it, which means doing what's right. Most business leaders are likely to hold themselves to higher standards in the absence of regulation than they would with it.

Besides, they can't take the judge and jury out to dinner and a ball game.

Bank deposit insurance, almost 70 years old, has enabled the enormous build-up of debt that is now so injurious to the nation's financial health. This brief comment is included in Chapter 2, The Biggest Hurt, but is repeated here because of its importance.

BANK DEPOSIT INSURANCE

Since 1933, the Federal Deposit Insurance Corporation has insured bank deposits. All deposit guarantees are a mistake. They induce depositors to care about a bank's interest rate and convenience, but not the money's safety. The guarantees enabled debt to expand for decades throughout the economy. Without them, big depositors would have insisted on the safety of their money, reducing the nation's level of debt.

FREE COLLEGE EDUCATION

January 29, 2018. From 1987 to 2010, the average net tuition for higher education, adjusted for inflation, rose 107%. The government paid enormous funds to colleges, also subsidizing and guaranteeing student loans. But the colleges raised tuitions anyway, making them less accessible to the poor.[27]

Colleges hired armies of administrators and built elaborate student centers with gorgeous swimming pools. But teaching turned into socialist indoctrination. Professors held America responsible for many of the world's problems, which is absurd. Racial issues were overplayed. Black studies and women's studies induced students to consider themselves victims. Students forcibly prevented speakers from expressing opinions the students considered discomforting, but the students were not expelled. As to students learning to become responsible, productive citizens, not so much.

Bernie Sanders now wants government to pay for all college education, increasing the demand and raising costs even more. Government officials would call the shots, making the mess all the worse.

Enough. Let's close the Department of Education, drop education subsidies, put more courses online, and cut tuitions.

More apprenticeship programs would enable young people not suited for college to learn a job and start earning money right off.

We also need more schools operating for profit. Profits, not government, provide the incentive for better results and lower costs.

TARIFFS: BAD IDEA

July 19, 2017. President Trump is considering a tariff on foreign steel imports. A tariff is a tax. It will cause U.S. unemployment to rise and U.S.

---

27. AIER, *Sorry, Bernie Bros, "Free" College Will Cost You.*

income to fall. Here's why:

The U.S. steel industry has 140,000 workers. U.S. companies that use steel have about six million workers – more than forty times more.

With a tariff imposed, the price of steel rises, making the prices of products that use steel rise as well. The increase lowers the demand for those products, causing some of the six million workers to be laid off.

The income lost by the laid-off employees of companies that *use* steel will outweigh the income gained by the employees of companies that *make* steel.

In addition, companies protected by tariffs generally stop innovating, preventing future prices from falling.

Tariffs cause more harm than good.

GET GOVERNMENT OUT OF DRUG TESTING

June 3, 2019. Government drug testing raises costs and costs lives.

A key goal of government officials is to avoid blame. Government testers have kept some drugs off the market for years to avoid blame for approving a drug that later proves unsafe. More lives have been lost from the delays than have been saved by ensuring drug safety.

Some patients face death if they don't receive an experimental drug soon.

Nope, say the feds. Can't have it. The drug might not be safe.

But without the drug, the patient will certainly die. With it, she may live.

Doesn't matter. Complying with the request goes against procedure.

Common sense is not a bureaucrat's best quality. If the patient dies because of the drug, the bureaucrat might be blamed. Better to rely on procedures and avoid making judgments.

Testing should be done by private testing companies. Companies would be sued if drugs are unsafe, of course. Testing is likely to be better when it's not performed by government. Costs, delays, and deaths are all reduced.

Government has no profits and no competition and doesn't fire incompetent workers. It's the most expensive way of doing anything.

Congress should limit the penalties for drugs that later prove unsafe and cause a lawsuit to be lost. Perfection is too expensive. It causes drugs to be held off the market for too long, resulting in unnecessary deaths.

In addition to safety, the government also tests whether a drug works better than the competition. But government doesn't test other products for efficacy. Why drugs?

Because government likes to exercise power whenever possible.

Judgments about efficacy would be better made by doctors, nurses, and patients, not testers.

Purchasers of cars face numerous choices of types and models. They don't need government telling them which one works best for them. Why not drugs? Getting government out of drug testing would save lives and cut costs. Nice combination.

GOVERNMENT DRUG TESTING HAS COST TOO MANY LIVES

July 10, 2017. Government is the worst choice for doing drug testing. When people want something done – and they certainly want their drugs tested, at least for safety – there's an opportunity for entrepreneurs. If one testing company performs poorly, the drug company would turn to a competitor.

Government officials have no competition. They value their work by the size of their budgets and the amount of power they have over others. As to drug testing, the biggest incentive is to avoid being blamed.

Let's say that drug testing is privatized. An array of companies are available to do the work, including even the drug companies themselves.

Some testers would do the most thorough job, charging high prices (but lower than government costs). Others would offer mid-level testing with modest prices. Still others would do minimal testing at minimal cost. For each drug, the pharmaceutical company could choose the level of testing it prefers, recognizing that the greater the risks, the higher the drug company's insurance premiums.

The consumers of drugs, their doctors and, when there's a lawsuit, the courts, should determine whether drugs are safe. After privatization, the pressure to cut costs would probably reduce the people's desire for ideal testing. Perfection is too expensive. The new standard would be reasonableness, which applies to the testing of most other products.

No one has counted how many lives have been taken too soon because the government kept effective drugs off the market for years to make sure it couldn't be blamed. Many more lives have been lost from those delays than have been saved by the government making certain drugs are safe and effective.

To perform any service, government is the worst choice.

GOVERNMENT LICENSING FOR SAFETY: BAD IDEA

Let's say that hairdressers are no longer licensed.

A customer is injured by a dye used to color her hair. She sues the hairdresser, the supplier, and the manufacturer of the dye. The press furnishes publicity. The industry and the public take notice. After several of these episodes, most people would become concerned about safety.

But the regulators want to prevent those several episodes. They like controlling the lives of others, and they're willing to make life harder for the poor to prevent a few extra safety problems, a wretched trade-off. Most people would learn to take safety into account and select the businesses that serve them by buying from some and not from others.

If an association of hairdressers forms to keep out competition, it should be sued. If an association forms to maintain a certain *quality* of hairdressing, a competing association could offer a different quality.

The government monopoly over licensing permits no competition. Licensing for safety, even the licensing of doctors, nurses, and lawyers, causes more harm than good. Let the buyers decide.

REPEAL FEDERAL FLOOD INSURANCE

October 12, 2017. In hurricane-prone areas, the risk of flooding is enormous. Insurance companies, in competition with one another, set the premiums as low as they can. But the premiums are high nonetheless because the risks are great. The premiums send a signal: Hurricanes are dangerous.

Prosperous seacoast homeowners complain to legislators that, without low flood-insurance premiums, they can't afford a home near the coast. The legislators should respond, "The premiums are high for good reason. We suggest you live elsewhere."

Legislators, you may have noticed, say nothing of the sort. They prefer to be reelected. Instead, they risk other people's money and offer insurance from the National Flood Insurance Program that sets premiums unrealistically low. For seacoast dwellers and the businesses that serve them, the benefits are obvious and substantial. The program also enables legislators to give the appearance that they care. They do care, but they care even more about reelection.

The costs? Seacoasts occasionally get whacked with billions of dollars of property damage. Paid by the federal government or added to the debt, the costs amount to just a few dollars per person for the 200 million Americans who live apart from the sea.

Suppose that U.S. senators and representatives are allowed to serve for only one term each. The homeowner says, "If you don't reduce my flood-insurance premiums, I'll vote you out of office."

The representative can respond, "That's okay. I'll be leaving anyway."

Bingo, the pressure to appease interest groups is reduced, and legislators can focus on the nation's long-term interests. Like repealing the National Flood Insurance Program.

THE JONES ACT: PROTECTIONISM IN ACTION[28]

January 27, 2020. Puerto Rico recently needed a shipment of liquid natural gas. Simple solution: Import it from nearby America, right?

Sorry, that would have been against U.S. law. The Puerto Rico shipment came from Siberia.

The less expensive solution was prevented by the Merchant Marine Act of 1920, usually known as the Jones Act. This requires that goods shipped between U.S. ports and territories must be carried on ships built in America, 75% owned and 75% crewed by Americans, and with the goods never sold to foreign citizens. The purpose: to protect American shipping. Ha! Lots of shipping to and from U.S. shores has been protected out of existence.

Ships built abroad cost far less than those that comply with the Jones Act. Repealing the law and using foreign-made ships would cut the cost and increase the volume of shipping to and from America, stimulating the U.S. economy.

The Seafarers International Union, representing U.S. merchant mariners sailing aboard U.S.-flagged vessels, supports the Jones Act with congressional campaign gifts. The union has 36,000 members. They're the winners. The U.S. has 328 million citizens. They're the losers.

The Jones Act has imposed significant costs on America. It's time for the members of Congress to assign the nation a higher priority than their own campaign coffers. It's time to give the Jones Act the deep six.

---

28. WSJ Editorial, 'America First'? Kill the Jones Act, 11/4/19.

PRIVATIZE THE POSTAL SERVICE

August 12, 2019. The U.S. Constitution authorizes the federal government to operate a postal service, but does not require it. Let's take advantage and get government out of the postal business.

The 630,000 U.S. postal employees are the world's highest-paid, semi-skilled workers. Privatization would save a bundle.

The price of a one-ounce, first-class letter is 55 cents, whether it's sent across the street or 7,894 miles from Concord, NH to Guam. This is nuts! Prices should be set according to costs.

With privatization, I'm guessing that a letter from New York City to Washington, DC would cost a dime. From a little town in New Hampshire to a little town in Montana, more like two dollars.

The four senators from New Hampshire and Montana would say, "That discriminates against the residents of our towns!"

Nonsense! Prices everywhere should be set according to costs. You, senators, are the discriminators. You enable the compensation of postal workers to be unnaturally high so you may receive campaign money from the union. If your time in office was limited to a single term, you wouldn't need to grovel for campaign contributions while in office. The job would be more fun. We want you to be happy in your work. But after six years, get out and go home.

Technology is rendering postal services obsolescent. Never mind 55-cent stamps; we can send emails for free. Postal deficits are growing. Covering them with taxes or piling them onto the federal deficit is outrageous.

The U.S. postal service should be privatized.

PRIVATIZE ALL SCHOOLS

Thomas Jefferson was wrong. Government should have nothing to do with education at any level. It should not own, operate, or fund schools, nor provide financial assistance to anyone attending school.

Government would be far more helpful to society if it stopped trying to be helpful. This doesn't mean we need no government. The eight essential duties government should perform are listed in Chapter 11.

Back to education. The dynamics of government that cause it to do so much harm in other areas apply also to education, particularly its excessive costs and the teaching of the supposed benefits of governmental force. As the inimitable Thomas Sowell put it, "Ideas that don't work are concentrated in institutions where ideas don't have to work to survive."

At universities, survive they do. It's not much of an exaggeration to cite a liberal belief that anyone other than healthy, heterosexual, white, Anglo-Saxon, Protestant men are probably victims of those who are. They want all such victims to be taken care of by our dear, caring, liberal government.

Grievance is a big deal in universities. So are safe-space demands, which prevent anyone from speaking or writing ideas that discomfort liberal children.

Most university faculty members are not fond of the U.S. Constitution. Like President Obama, they feel the Constitution imposes limits on the force they think government should apply.

Universities provide tenure to some of their faculty members, meaning that such professors can't be fired. People who are subject to being fired at least keep one leg on the ground to make sure they have some contact with reality. Professors with tenure can fly into the blue, like helium-filled balloons, with ideas that have not the slightest resemblance to reality.

All schools should be owned by individuals or corporations in the private sector, for profit or not for profit. Some teaching might be done by older students teaching younger students. Schools should be funded by tuitions or gifts. After a time (and with very low tax rates), I would expect wealthy individuals to compete with one another as to who provides the most to inner city schools.

DRAINING THE SWAMP

December 2, 2019. A Republican running for Congress promises to cut back government and is elected. But he casts liberal votes and becomes a Republican-in-Name-Only. The swamp has swallowed him up.

Before the Civil War, people obtained federal jobs by actively supporting or raising money for candidates who won. The "spoils system" was overtly corrupt, but the bureaucracy was small, had little power, and was uprooted by elections every few years.

The Pendleton Civil Service Reform Act of 1883 created a permanent, merit-based bureaucracy. It now numbers 2.8 million individuals, with salaries and benefits greatly exceeding those of people with equivalent private sector jobs.

The November 16, 2019 article from AIER, *Birth of the Deep State: A History*, written by economist Peter C. Earle, contains a fascinating description of the federal bureaucracy. I quote parts of it here:

The major functions of the bureaucracy are "to thwart political measures it collectively deems unpalatable and to vigilantly protect the existence of the greater body within which it thrives.

"No orders are issued, and there is no chain of command. It communicates by example: leaks reported in the news beget more leaks; anonymous tips spawn a rash of new tipsters. No lofty conspiracy theories are necessary; a massive army of bureaucrats in an era of free/highly affordable burner phones, file sharing services, and document-scanning apps are more than sufficient to gum up the wheels of executive action.

"There are no secret codes, no dead drops, and no shadowy agents meeting in parking garages in the dead of night. Perhaps more dauntingly, the deep state coalesces from among a seemingly incalculable number of nondescript men and women with families and homes in the Virginia and Maryland suburbs of Washington, DC. (The deep state) receives a salary every two weeks, drawn upon the United States Treasury. Its atomic elements – individuals – coach Little League, go to Zumba classes, and generally have mainstream opinions. Many, no doubt, dismiss the very notion of a deep state. Even when they send an anonymous email, shred a document intended for other eyes, or impishly pass a tip to someone with a second- or third-hand relationship in the media, most of them probably see the deep state as something larger, above and beyond themselves.

"Yet they are the deep state."

This is me again. Not having profits by which to measure their self-esteem, bureaucrat managers rate themselves by the size of their budgets, the number of people working for them, and how much power they wield. As demonstrated in the article above, bureaucrats have numerous ways of securing policies that benefit themselves. The corruption is indirect, but it's massive.

Via laws and regulations, the government uses force to excess. The intended purposes are benign, and potential problems are unseen. But in the long run, governmental force nearly always causes far more harm than good.

The welter of laws and regulations makes voters unable to link the damage with the policies that caused it. More laws are passed to redress the harm, and yet more problems result. The gargantuan government raises frustration and costs and lowers morale.

Today's bureaucracy is much more damaging than that of the spoils system. It's time to trash the Civil Service System and drain the swamp.

Some protest that the complexity of modern life requires a large government.

Nonsense! The people of America possess ever-greater expertise. If free markets were allowed to operate with minimal government intervention, the benefits of that expertise would permeate the entire nation, especially benefiting the poor.

MORE ON THE SWAMP

July 30, 2018: President Trump and the courts are starting to drain the swamp. Federal bureaucrats, numbering more than two million, constitute the swamp. The president has direct authority over just 2% of these bureaucrats. Until a recent decision by the Supreme Court, some of them, unconfirmed by the Senate, interpreted and enforced laws and regulations, sometimes imposing serious penalties.

A Department of Education "guidance letter" stripped male college students of due process when accused of sexual misconduct. Mr. Trump has repealed that letter.

Until recently, it took six to twelve months to remove a poor-performing bureaucrat and another eight months to resolve appeals, with the individual being paid all along. At the Department of Veterans Affairs, more than 470 employees, including doctors and nurses, spend all their working time on union activities. Some have spent so little time treating patients that they've lost their certification and can no longer see patients. Yet they continue to be paid as professionals. President Trump has partially corrected these abuses.

More civil servants die on the job than are terminated or demoted. The fastest way for a bureaucracy to remove itself is to solve problems. This they try to avoid.

Including benefits, the average private sector worker in 2016 earned $69,901. The average federal worker earned $123,160 – 76% higher. Controlling the lives of common folks who don't work for government must be tough work.

The deep state has been growing in size and power for more than a century. Fortunately, a reversal has begun.

TAME THE ADMINISTRATIVE STATE[29]

January 15, 2019. Past Supreme Court decisions, mistakenly, have helped make the administrative state become larger and more intrusive.

In the 1984 *Chevron* case, the justices directed lower courts to defer to the federal agencies in their interpretations of Congressional laws.

In the 1997 *Auer* case, the justices directed lower courts to defer to the federal agencies regarding interpretations by the agencies of their own regulations.

Government is naturally inclined to expand its powers. The U.S. government has gone way overboard, partly because of *Chevron* and *Auer*. In the last 25 years, U.S. agencies have issued never fewer than 3,000 rules and enforcements each year, making unelected bureaucrats America's primary lawgivers.

The Supreme Court has now accepted a case in which it will review the *Auer* case. The court would be wise to reverse it, and eventually reverse *Chevron* as well.

America's founding fathers had experienced the tyranny that resulted when a single person or agency not only made laws, but also interpreted, administered, and enforced the laws. The more concentrated government's powers, the worse conditions become for citizens, especially the poor. Take Venezuela, for example.

The founders wisely split the powers: They planned for Congress to make the laws, the judiciary to interpret them, and the executive to administer and enforce them.

America's administrative agencies have concentrated those powers

---

29. WSJ, Peter J. Wallison, *The Supreme Court May Begin to Tame the Administrative State,* 12/14/18.

in themselves. It's time for them to be reined in. Reversing *Chevron* and *Auer* would help.

Bureaucrats in Arms[30]

March 25, 2019. America's federal bureaucracy is well supplied with weaponry. The U.S. Government Accountability Office reports that, from 2010 to 2017, 20 non-military, "law enforcement" agencies spent at least $38.8 million on firearms, $325.9 million on ammunition, and $1.14 billion on tactical equipment.

By 2017, the IRS had 4,487 guns, including 15 fully automatic machine guns and 5.1 million rounds of ammunition. Machine guns, of course, are essential when you're auditing taxpayers.

The Health and Human Services Office of the Inspector General had 194 fully automatic firearms and 386,952 rounds of ammo. Inspector generalship is always dangerous.

The EPA had 377 pistols with 220,418 pistol rounds and 223 shotguns with 146,975 shotgun rounds. Those dirty polluters, you gotta watch 'em every minute.

The FDA had 390 pistols with 166,783 pistol rounds and 122 shotguns with 30,620 shotgun rounds. Without being armed, inspecting meat and researching drugs is foolhardy.

Yes, the weapons are critical and fully justified. The deplorables may launch an attack any day.

The New Zealand mosque where worshipers were slaughtered had only one exit – the very door where the gunman stood. But if some members of the congregation had carried guns, the gunman would have been shot after only a few parishioners had been killed, not 50. The more guns, the less crime.

America's bureaucracy, however, is taking things a little too far.

---

30. Newsmax, Bill Hoffmann, *Govt. Agencies Buying Thousands of Guns,* February 2019.

You remember the stirring end of the Gettysburg Address: "We highly resolve that government of the bureaucrats, by the bureaucrats, and for the bureaucrats shall not perish from the earth."

Well, that's what Lincoln said, wasn't it?

THE NATIONAL DEBT CANNOT GROW FOREVER

November 18, 2019: The national debt cannot accumulate indefinitely. Eventually, the whatchamacallit hits the fan.

People who limit their consumption don't accumulate debt. Americans haven't limited their consumption, but they certainly have accumulated debt. The national debt is already 28% higher than the entire year's gross domestic production.

Current Americans expect future Americans to limit *their* consumption to repay it – a sweet dream that won't come true. Future Americans won't bear the brunt of other people's profligacy. They will reject higher taxes to cover the debt.

Liberals blithely say, "The debt doesn't matter. We owe it to ourselves."[31] That doesn't include the liberals, of course. They're too busy thinking up ways of adding to it. They want power, and they want control of the flow of money that goes with the power. Nothing else counts.

Well, defeating Trump ranks right up there.

If the debt continues to grow faster than the economy, the federal government will eventually go bankrupt. We would join the crowd of six nations whose runaway inflation since 1945 has made their savings worthless.[32] Social Security and Medicare payments would stop. Banks and insurance companies would go under. Widespread bankruptcy would prevail, and consumption would fall sharply. It would be a miserable time, and Jews would probably get the blame.

31. Scott Burns, *National Debt: We Owe It to Ourselves?* I don't know where I got the piece from – possibly AIER.
32. I recall obtaining this information from the Web.

Is there a happier scenario?

Yes. To pay the debt, the U.S. government should auction to private interests the enormous amount of land it owns but does not use. It should also coordinate with other nations to sell to private interests the world's oceans and polar caps.

To keep debt from rebuilding, the members of Congress should be limited to a single term, the Civil Service System should be terminated, the Federal Reserve Bank should be abolished, and spending by America's government sector should be reduced by 90%. That'll do nicely.

The huge debts would not quickly disappear. They would transfer from the government to the private interests who acquired those assets. But as the purchases are digested by the private parties over time, the debts would diminish. Government debts seldom diminish.

INTEREST ON THE NATIONAL DEBT

August 26, 2019: The U.S. Treasury currently pays interest on the $22 trillion national debt at a low rate: 1.8%. The interest payments this year total $389 billion. Full-time U.S. workers number about 132 million. The $389 billion payments represent almost $3,000 for each worker.

If and when interest rates eventually double or triple, the interest payments would amount to…well, real money.

And if the debt itself continues to rise? But there's no chance of that, right?[33]

---

33. But there's a good chance the debt will indeed rise. If it does, and interest rates go up as well because of higher inflation, the burden would be far beyond the government's capacity to deal with it. The interest burden could approach one-third of government's total expenditures, forcing the government to borrow or create money just to pay the interest. Bankruptcy would follow.

GOVERNMENTS SHOULD SELL THE LAND IT DOES NOT ITSELF UTILIZE

January 13, 2020. All U.S. governments (but mostly the feds) should sell the land they own but do not utilize themselves. Forests, rivers, mountains, parks, prairies, reservoirs, aquifers, swamps, deserts, tundra, and national parks should be auctioned to the highest bidders. About 80% of Nevada and 60% of Utah would go. Military bases would be retained; Indian reservations would not. Radioactive land would sell cheap.

Most national parks would continue as tourist attractions. But with private ownership, the management would improve and the costs would fall.

All sources of fresh water should be privately owned.

If a corporation owned a portion of the Mississippi River, it could earn money from those who use the waters for transportation, irrigation, manufacturing, fishing, drinking, or recreation. If a river owner allows her portion of the Mississippi to become polluted, the downstream owner would sue. If the river's mouth is polluted, the owner of that portion of the Gulf of Mexico would sue. Monitoring pollution is cheaper than lawsuits, making lawsuits infrequent.

Most timber owners prefer steady income and do not clear-cut their trees. Most privately owned forests are cleared of debris and suffer few forest fires.

Government should reserve whatever reasonable portions of the spectrum it needs for the military and the police and then sell the rest to the highest bidders. Thereafter, if the government needs more spectrum, it would have to pay for it.

Corporations and most private owners take into account long-term prospects, including the interests of descendants, as well as short-term prospects. Government's time horizon extends mostly to the next election.

For private parties, competition and press publicity reduce waste and wrongdoing. Having no competition, government is permeated with waste and wrongdoing, much of it hidden.

A matrix of private ownership would protect the environment and preserve values far better than government.

PRIVATIZE ROADS AND BRIDGES

A friend asked, "Would you want to sell even the roads?"

You bet I would. Interstates, bridges, streets, and roads should all be sold to the highest bidders. Privatizing government services invariably improves quality and lowers costs.

The transition could take years. The new owners would probably implant electronic devices on or inside the surface of streets, roads, and bridges. Owners of vehicles would be required to install corresponding electronics. The road's owner would then know that your car has been on that road or that bridge. She would also know the vehicle's weight, the weather conditions, and the time of day, and would charge your bank account or credit card accordingly. Charges would increase if you drive during busy commuter hours. The total cost of roads would fall. Some of them would probably be freebies.

An owner would set the rules of the road and could either set up a police force or rent a government police force.

The primary cause of road deterioration is heavy trucks. But the trucking companies currently avoid most of the road repair costs. The federal, state, and local governments pay, adding to tax bills. If the roads were sold to private parties, the truckers would be charged realistically, and taxes would fall.

Higher trucking costs would mean fewer trucks. But more goods could then be carried by rail. On long trips, rail is cheaper than trucks, causing the prices of goods to fall as well.

Privatizing the roads would set prices according to costs. We'd enjoy better roads and save money to boot.

CHAPTER 4 – THE LOCKDOWNS

LOCKING EVERYONE DOWN: WRETCHED POLICY

APRIL 6, 2020. STRANGLING THE economy to protect against the coronavirus causes bankruptcies, money shortages, excessive debt, untreated illnesses, loneliness, inactivity, overeating, alcoholism, domestic violence, and other problems that can result in depression, deaths, and even suicides.

Also, the constraint of supply, coupled with government's massive stimulation of demand, will probably cause higher prices.

For older people, isolated care is fine. But for most others, the best defense is to be exposed to the virus to develop immunity. Without immunity, a second wave of the disease is likely if and when people again co-mingle. If you're 70 and under, in good physical condition, you should probably get out and about.

California has far fewer coronavirus deaths than New York, possibly because California had many visitors from China from December on and developed immunity.

Sweden remains open, using a laissez-faire, targeted approach and not decimating the economy. (To have done otherwise would have been prevented by Sweden's Constitution.) Influenced by frequent expert advice, the people themselves decide what they'll do. Sweden's coronavirus deaths, divided by the total population, are higher than that of the U.S. (.0047% versus .0029%). But the percentages for both countries, as you can see, are infinitesimal.

Italy has Europe's oldest population and the most smokers. So having the highest rate of coronavirus deaths is no coincidence. Worldwide, deaths *with* the coronavirus are far more numerous than deaths *caused* by it.

At this writing on April 6, 2020, U.S. coronavirus deaths, according to Worldometers, number 9,624. Eventual reported deaths will likely fit into the yearly range of panic-free influenza deaths, namely, 30,000-45,000. Imprudent Fed projections, currently up to 240,000 deaths, result only in panic.

The Spanish Flu in 1918 was deadlier than the current virus. Yet the U.S. economy was affected hardly at all because the government did almost nothing about it. Now, the panic aroused by government's intrusions and its other policies will cause a serious economic downturn. Current medical science would have been able to handle the current crisis without help. Big government usually causes more harm than good. Widespread lockdowns are nuts!

LOCKDOWNS AND MASKS MAKE NO DIFFERENCE

August 26, 2020. A working paper by the National Bureau of Economic Research (NBER) as of late July analyzes countries and U.S. states with more than 1,000 Covid-19 deaths. The study included 23 countries and 25 U.S. states.

Whether or not governments required lockdowns, travel restrictions, masks, or curfews, the results were the same: Once the region suffered a total of 25 Covid-19 deaths, the number of deaths per day stopped increasing within a month thereafter.[34] The rate of immunization seems to apply everywhere. (The conclusions clearly do not apply to India's 1.4 billion people as a whole. The study probably did not include India.)

Another study: TrendMacro found that at the very least, "heavy lockdowns were no more effective than light ones. It also found that opening up a lot was no more harmful than opening up a little."[35]

OPEN LETTER FROM BELGIUM[36]

September 20, 2020. A lengthy open letter about the pandemic, signed so far by 394 Belgian medical doctors, 1,340 medically trained health professionals, and 8,897 citizens, was recently sent to Belgium authorities. Here are some of the highlights:

- The more social and emotional commitments people have, the more resistant they are to viruses. But lockdowns and quarantines reduced social and economic commitments.

- Physical activity improves physical health, energy levels, and quality of life and reduces depression and anxiety. But isolation reduced physical activity.

- Social distancing has increased fear, persistent stress, and loneliness, cutting general and psychological health.

- The vast majority of deceased patients has been 80 years old or older. Most of the deceased who were younger had underlying disorders, including obesity. Statistics have not taken into account that death by coronavirus is different from death *with* corona.

- Over 98% of those infected by the coronavirus hardly became ill. Mortality rates have been close to those of normal seasonal flu.

---

34. AIER, Stephen C. Miller, *Lockdowns and Mask Mandates Do Not Lead to Reduced COVID Transmission Rates or Deaths, New Study Suggests,* 8/26/20.
35. WSJ, Donald L. Luskin, *The Failed Experiment of Covid Lockdowns,* 9/2/20.
36. AIER Staff, *Open Letter from Medical Doctors and Health Professionals,* 9/20/20.

- For those showing severe corona symptoms, hydroxychloro-quine (HCQ), zinc, and azithromycin (AZT) have been effective, affordable, and safe.

- The waves of infection in countries with strict lockdowns are similar to those without. Lockdowns have not reduced mortality rates.

- Transmission of the virus occurs by aerosols or by coughing and sneezing in closed, unventilated rooms. The virus does not transmit between people who have tested positive but are asymptomatic. In the open air, contamination is impossible. There is no scientific proof that transmission occurs via money or other objects.

- Oral masks are appropriate for hospitals, retirement homes, and at-risk groups. But for healthy individuals, they are unnecessary. Oral masks create oxygen deficiencies, with effects similar to altitude sickness. The accumulation of CO_2 inside masks can cause toxic acidification, which reduces immunity. A mask creates an environment that is poorly ventilated.

- Second coronavirus waves "exist" only because the number of tests increased. Without the additional testing, there would have been no second coronavirus waves. Deaths and hospitalizations did not increase. (I would add: The number of infections don't matter because more than 99% of them have little or no consequence. When testing started, deaths and hospitalizations had already peaked. The testing was a waste of money. Testing is not done for normal seasonal flu, and no one misses it.)

- In ten years of influenza, vaccinations have had limited effects. For those over 75 years old, the efficiency of vaccination is almost non-existent.

- Social isolation and economic damage have increased depression, anxiety, suicides, intra-family violence, and child abuse.

Emergency coronavirus policies have been extremely damaging and are medically unjustified, like using a sledgehammer to crack a nut. Normal democratic governance and all civil liberties should immediately be restored.

THE GREAT BARRINGTON DECLARATION

October 8, 2020. Written by three prominent epidemiologists, the Great Barrington Declaration is signed by 4,819 medical and public health scientists, 9,084 medical practitioners, and 126,160 members of the general public (plus one – me). The declaration is sponsored by the American Institute of Economic Research, which is located in Great Barrington, Massachusetts.

The declaration says that current lockdowns are producing devastating effects on short- and long-term public health, including worsening cardiovascular disease outcomes, fewer cancer screenings, and deteriorating mental health. The lockdowns are leading to excess mortality in years to come. With schools closed, the young will carry heavy burdens, and so will the working class. Keeping the measures in place until a vaccine is available "will cause irreparable damage, with the underprivileged disproportionately harmed."

The vulnerability to death from Covid-19 is more than a thousandfold higher in the old and infirm than in the young. Those who are at high risk should have "focused protection," but those who are at minimal risk of death should live normal lives to build immunity. All schools should be open for in-person teaching. Extracurricular activities, such as sports, should be resumed. Low-risk adults should work normally, rather than from home. Restaurants and other businesses should open. Arts, music, and other cultural activities should resume. Over time, people who have gained immunity will immunize the aged and infirm.

WHY BUREAUCRATS ARE WRONG
ABOUT THE PANDEMIC

April 13, 2020. Politicians are relying on bureaucrats to deal with the pandemic. But the dynamics of government usually make them wrong for the following reasons:

- Since government has no profits, bureaucrats find other ways to measure their self-worth. The bigger the budget, the better. Recommendations by them are likely to include a larger role for government. They remain unaware that a larger role for government generally causes more harm than good.

- They do their utmost to avoid being blamed and are inclined to go along with the majority of experts. The majority of experts are wrong surprisingly often. They certainly were this time around.

- Bureaucrats exaggerate their projections about the pandemic, fomenting panic, which induces people to follow their advice.

- Government employees are the only people permitted to exercise force. Bureaucrats are paid more than those with equivalent jobs in the private sector and cannot be fired. With a "we-they" attitude, they have little empathy for the ill effects of the force they apply.

- Bureaucrats are generally uncomfortable with free markets because free markets empower people outside of government. The bureaucrats prefer to have the power themselves. The more the government exercises power, the weaker the economy becomes. But the weakening is not of great concern to the bureaucrats. They can't be fired. Also, the economy's complexity enables them to find someone else to blame.

- Bureaucrats prefer not to actually *solve* social and economic problems because this would render their jobs unnecessary. Whatever extends a problem suits their interest, as long they can avoid blame.

- Even though older people may have the virus in their bodies, the majority die from other causes. Bureaucrats nevertheless report such deaths as coronavirus deaths, generating additional panic and attracting attention to themselves.

Rather than trust bacteria to quickly develop immunity, bureaucrats have forced people to remain at home, grinding down the economy. Widespread immunity is delayed, and countless unnecessary deaths will result. For many citizens, the lockdowns are catastrophic. With little empathy, the bureaucrats justify themselves, "Oh, we're just trying to save lives."

Nonsense! To save lives, everyone except those who are unhealthy or over 70 should conduct life normally. For any respiratory pandemic, the best solution is for children in school and healthy people under 70 to mingle and develop herd immunity. Some may develop minor symptoms, but few will die. After as little as four weeks, the disease would die, and the people who had been isolated could join with the rest.[37]

Ah, but this happier scenario provides no opportunity for the bureaucrats to make a big deal of themselves and exercise force.

SWEDEN AND U.S. UPDATE

April 20, 2020. So far, Sweden has had 1,580 reported coronavirus deaths, which is 154 deaths per million population.

The United States has had 40,565 reported coronavirus deaths, or 124 deaths per million population. Both percentages are tiny. Sweden's death rate is higher, but Sweden has kept its economy open.

---

37. AIER, Edward Peter Stringham, *Stand Up for Your Rights, says Professor Knut M. Wittkowski,* 4/6/20.

The U.S. has not. Emotionally and economically, the U.S. lockdowns have been catastrophic. After this is over, I expect we'll learn that the U.S. lockdowns have caused more deaths than the lives they've saved – certainly a tremendous amount of worry and unhappiness.

The government could have allowed people to decide for themselves whether they're vulnerable to the virus. Those who deemed themselves healthy could have worked, mingled, and become immune.

Oh no, you can't trust just plain people to make decisions as important as that.

Knut Wittkowski, PhD, has been an epidemiological modeler for 35 years. He heads the Department of Biostatistics, Epidemiology, and Research Design at New York's Rockefeller University.

In an American Institute of Economic Research article,[38] Wittkowski said the only thing that stops all respiratory diseases is herd immunity. About 80% of the people need to have contact with the virus. The majority won't even know they were infected or they'll have mild symptoms.

Elderly people should be separated and nursing homes closed. But schools should be kept open. After about four weeks, herd immunity will have been attained, and life can return to normal.

LOCKDOWNS DECIMATE LIBERTY

May 18, 2020. Nan wrote, "Sweden has three times the death rate of its neighbors! Sweden's 'herd immunity' has failed."

Actually, the number of Sweden's COVID-19 deaths is *more* than three times higher than that of its neighbors. But Sweden recognizes the damage caused by lockdowns. Its efforts have not failed.

Last year, Sweden had 13,757 *influenza* deaths. That was almost four times greater than Sweden's current COVID-19 deaths. You weren't dis-

---

38. Ibid.

turbed by the influenza number, were you, Nan? I didn't think so.[39]

Lockdowns damage the whole society, but especially the poor.[40] A recent survey by the Federal Reserve Bank found the layoffs hit low-wage U.S. workers the hardest:

- Among households earning less than $40,000 a year, a damaging 39% experienced at least one job loss in March.

- Among households earning between $40,000 and $100,000, only 19% suffered one job loss (down from 39% above).

- For households earning more than $100,000, a piddling 13% had one job loss.

Yes, lockdowns are another wonderful way for government to help the poor.

Unfortunately, President Trump so far has given voice to government epidemiologists who have created panic and focused on saving lives at all costs from the beginning. This plays into the hands of Democrats and the media, who want the economy to deteriorate so much that they can defeat Trump in November. (By October, however, Mr. Trump has begun to encourage state governors to knock off the lockdowns.)

Other epidemiologists – prominent epidemiologists Knut Wittkowski and John Ioannidis, for example – have not been given much voice. They believe that only older people should be isolated. Everyone else should go to work and school, mingling and developing immunity. After a time, the immune can immunize older people. In the long run, this saves the most lives, not to mention the economy.

Neither the government nor most of the media sought the advice of Messrs. Wittkowski or Ioannidis about the pandemic. It did not suit their interests.

---

39. All along, I have obtained information about coronavirus deaths from www.worldometers.info.

40. Forbes, Tommy Beer, *Covid-19 Fallout: Lower-Income Earners Hit Hardest by Job Losses,* 5/14/20.

WSJ, David Harrison, *Low-Wage Workers Hit Harder by Layoffs,* 5/15/20.

In 1968, during a flu pandemic that killed 100,000 Americans, people didn't think of locking down. They went to Woodstock instead. Americans have grown soft. They want government to take care of them.

Out of the 328 million U.S. population, fewer than one hundred people under 24 have died from COVID-19.[41] Why the absurd school closings?

Night after night, TV news programs show deceased persons being trundled to morgues. Rarely mentioned is that the average age of death is over 80.

People understandably want to preserve lives. But they have far too little desire to preserve liberty. Lockdowns decimate liberty.

BIG SUCCESSES

(The following was written in May, 2020.) The lockdowns are causing deaths from delayed surgery and hospital visits, child molestation by intoxicated parents, spousal abuse, weakened immune systems, anxiety, suicides, renewed deaths when the lockdowns end, and a big step toward national bankruptcy.

Otherwise, they're just wonderful.

REVERSE-NEUTRON BOMB

May 25, 2020. A neutron bomb kills people but leaves buildings intact. An article published by the American Institute for Economic Research (AIER)[42] characterizes the COVID-19 lockdown as a *reverse*-neutron bomb. It kills the economy, but leaves people intact.

Well, it's intended to leave people intact. Actually, it leaves people

---

41. Washington Times, Richard W. Rahn, *Seen and Not Seen.* (Don't have a date.)
42. AIER, James Bovard, *Will the Political Class be Held Liable for What They've Done?* 5/21/20.

poorer, debt-ridden, depressed, alcoholic, and suicidal. Otherwise, they're just fine.

A surge of deaths approaches. Not from COVID-19. Oh no, the deaths will result from the lockdowns. People are missing medical screenings and checkups. They're not seeking treatment for early symptoms of illness, such as cancer. Too many unessential operations have been delayed to make way for coronavirus patients (which didn't materialize). Some of those unessential operations have become essential, and some will be too late. Unnecessary deaths caused by our cockeyed leadership may rival coronavirus deaths.

To prevent COVID-19 contagion, politicians have claimed the right to inflict unlimited economic damage on the American people. The Disaster Distress Helpline, a federal hotline, received nine times more phone calls in March than it did in March the year prior.

Unfortunately, politicians have no liability for the economic damage they foster.

New York Governor Andrew Cuomo ordered nursing homes to accept COVID-19 patients. This ignorant mandate resulted in some 5,000 nursing home deaths.

Pennsylvania's Health Secretary Dr. Rachel Levine issued a similar order, causing thousands of nursing home deaths. (But to keep her dear, 95-year-old mother safe, Dr. Levine removed her from a nursing home.)

Even though most COVID-19 infections were concentrated in the Detroit area, Michigan's Governor Gretchen Whitmer prohibited citizens from buying seeds for spring planting (initially, no lottery tickets). She prohibited everyone in the entire state from leaving their homes to visit family or friends, including in the northern counties that had near-zero infections and no fatalities.

Oregon Governor Kate Brown banned residents from leaving their homes except for essential work, buying food, and other narrow exemptions. She also banned all recreational travel. This was at a time when the state had few if any COVID-19 cases. Almost 400,000 Oregonians lost their jobs after Brown's shutdown.

Kentucky Governor Andy Beshear's shutdown paralyzed the state, even though COVID-19's impact in Kentucky, according to Senator Rand Paul, "has been no worse than an average flu season."

Politicians are expected to be informed, exercise reasonable judgment, and reflect empathy for difficulties their requirements may cause the citizens. Officials such as Cuomo, Levine, Whitmer, Brown, and Beshear – Democrats all – did none of those things. They should be held liable. They should be rendered as poor as church mice, scurrying on the floor for crumbs.

GOVERNMENT DYNAMICS HAVE CREATED LOCKDOWN DISASTERS

Without government involvement, people left on their own to deal with COVID-19 would have sifted through information from conflicting sources. The elderly and those with health issues would have isolated themselves. Everyone else would have gone to work and the children to school, to mingle, become infected, and develop immunity. After a few weeks, they would have rendered everyone else immune.

Those things didn't happen because of government's heavy involvement.

Right from the start, U.S. politicians and bureaucrats latched onto outrageous predictions about huge numbers of coronavirus deaths. They created panic and focused attention on themselves, enabling them to impose unnecessary and disastrous lockdowns.

It seemed evident from the start that, although COVID-19 was more contagious than most viruses, it was less deadly. But the politicians and bureaucrats focused their attention on the contagious aspect and disregarded the non-deadly. They get their kicks out of exercising force, and they pursued saving lives at all costs – other people's costs, of course. In all of American history, never has force been imposed so broadly on its citizens with such an outrageous loss of liberty.

The politicians and bureaucrats didn't want to render their jobs unnecessary. Contagion and immunization among younger people is the best and shortest path to dealing with viruses. But no, government tried to prevent contagion from occurring in the first place. This has delayed and is continuing to delay herd immunity, causing the pandemic to last longer. It will result in a new surge of deaths when the lockdowns are released.

The authorities have advised even young people to practice social distancing. What? Young people are highly unlikely to die from the coronavirus. They should mingle, up close and personal, to hasten immunization. Preventing contagion is like trying to stop the rain during a thunderstorm.

The dynamics of government have made our politicians and bureaucrats disastrously wrong. Their lockdown policies have also been highly unconstitutional.

LOCKDOWNS DEVASTATE THE POOR WORLDWIDE

World Bank President David Malpass observes[43] that the world's poorest countries are devastated by the shutdown of Western economies. It's not a question of when the pandemic subsides. What matters is when the advanced economies reopen.

Some 60 million people, the World Bank estimates, are likely to fall into extreme poverty this year, meaning they would subsist on less than $1.90 a day. Hundreds of millions could lose their jobs. The growth of millions of children could be stunted by inadequate nutrition.

---

43. WSJ, Paul Kiernan, *Coronavirus Shutdowns Wreak Devastating Toll on Poorest Nations*, 5/19/20.

Liberal politicians pride themselves on caring for the poor and endeavor to do this by exercising force, such as lockdowns. Freeing up the economy instead? Naah, that doesn't fit the template. As to the people in destitute countries, shoot, they don't matter; they don't vote here.

Lockdowns of nations in the Southern Hemisphere have been more stringent than in the U.S. While we're heading into summer, they're entering the cold weather of winter, which will increase the impact of the coronavirus. Many of their citizens believe that the disease represents a failure of capitalism.

Now there's a great idea. Get rid of free markets. You'll be on your way to happiness. Look no further than Venezuela. They shook off their free markets, and Venezuelan citizens are jumping with joy!

LURCHING[44]

After causing a serious and unnecessary economic downturn, officials are lurching too far the other way, paying out-of-work people so much that there's no need for them to return to work.

Under the Cares Act, hurriedly passed with other COVID-19 bills, people unemployed by the lockdown are entitled to receive $600 a week. This was targeted to generate 100% of mean earnings. But for those whose earnings were lower than the mean, $600 is an overpayment.

Some 68% of laid-off workers are now making more than they did on the job. One in five is making twice as much, and the bottom 10%, mostly part-timers, are collecting three times as much.

Retail workers are generally making 42% more by not working.

Janitors in companies that have remained open receive no hazard pay. But janitors of companies that shut down can collect more than 1½ times their prior wage.

In New Mexico, half the laid-off workers will make 77% more.

44. WSJ Editorial, *How to Keep Workers Off the Job*, 5/22/20.

If the overpayments aren't corrected soon, the economic recovery will be significantly delayed because companies will be unable to hire enough workers.

Officials are lurching from one side to the other, like first-time canoers caught in a storm. If they had just stopped getting involved from the start...

Are you kidding? Liberals will probably fight to retain the overpayments in hopes of continued economic weakness so that people will be more likely to vote liberal.

You mean liberals are more interested in being elected than they are in supporting a healthy economy? Say it's not so.

It's so. Liberals also like having people depend on them.

When people are not working, where will they get the money?

From rich people.

That's a one-time shot. After rich people's money is taken and spent, where will funding come from thereafter?

We'll worry about that when the time comes.

TRAGEDIES

During the pandemic, doctors in northern California have seen more deaths from suicide than they've seen from the coronavirus.[45]

Dr. Mike deBoisblanc, of the John Muir Medical Center in Walnut Creek, CA, told ABC 7 News that in the previous four weeks, he'd seen a year's worth of suicides.

By late March in one Tennessee county, more people had died from suicide than had died from the virus in the entire state.

Never mind. Officials assure us that the lockdowns are all about saving lives.

---

45. AIER, Jeffrey A. Tucker, *Lockdown Suicide Data Reveal Predictable Tragedy,* 5/22/20.

VIOLENCE BEGETS VIOLENCE[46]

June 2, 2020. America is now shaken by an explosion of violence in the streets.

And why not? The nation has been subject to the greatest act of violence ever inflicted on the American people by its government.

You can't go to work outside the home, say the officials; we've closed the businesses. If the owner keeps it open, we'll jail him. You can't go to church; we'll fine you. You can't get that toothache fixed; we've closed down the dentist. You can't undergo that unessential operation; you have to wait until it becomes essential and you're nearer to death. You can't gather and see friends; you have to remain lonely. Try not to hurt the kids.

We didn't cause all that street violence, the officials say. We're just trying to save lives.

You know not what you do. You see only your policy goals. Blinders keep you from seeing the indirect and long-term consequences. The rioting isn't even a long-term consequence, but still you don't see it.

Violence begets violence. You in government have become enemies of the people.

HERD IMMUNITY

June 12, 2020. Only two ways can COVID-19 be defeated: a vaccine and 80% herd immunity.

American has neither one. Herd immunity would already have prevailed except for the widespread government lockdowns.

Worldometer now reports there have been 116,035 COVID-19 deaths. With the lockdowns starting to lift and too few people immunized, deaths are now surging.

---

46. AIER, Jeffrey A. Tucker, *Here is What Happened to Social Harmony,* 10/7/18.

How many COVID-19 deaths would have been caused if the U.S. government had done nothing except provide good advice?

Ha!

Let's see: Epidemiologists John Ioannidis and Knut Wittkowski gave advice from the beginning that seemed sensible to me, as follows:

Lockdowns should have applied to everyone 65 and older – 14.9% of the population. (Elsewhere in this book, based on evidence I've read, I have changed the age of those who are especially vulnerable to 70 and older.)

Those who are younger but not in good shape (especially the obese) might also have chosen to stay inside.

This meant that some 80% of the people should have gotten out and mingled, up close and personal. No facemasks. No social distancing. No testing. Infection invited. Kissing encouraged. Children in school. Few would have died. Most would have been unaware they'd been infected.

In about a month, the disease would have run out of potential candidates and died. The immune could then have mingled with the older folks and immunized them as well.

The economy would have suffered a mere blip. No unusual misery, bankruptcy, alcoholism, child abuse, deaths from delayed medical care, or suicide. Possibly 40,000 actual U.S. coronavirus deaths. No multitude of deaths in third world countries because of slowdowns in the West. No unconstitutional abrogation of freedom. No unusual anger and rioting caused by the excessive use of government force.

We were just trying to save lives, say the officials.

Oh sure, you imbecilic royal highnesses. What you've done is abominable!

OLDER FOLKS ISOLATED

July 13, 2020: I suggested to Anne that, except for people 70 and older, widespread lockdowns should never have occurred. The children should have gone to school, and healthy people under 70 to work. People should have mingled and invited infection, promoting immunity. Within a month or two, herd immunity would have prevailed. Devoid of potential candidates for the disease, COVID-19 would long since have died.

Anne replied that the younger people would have infected the older ones, who would have died in great numbers.

A knowledgeable friend tells me there is "absolutely zero evidence of spread from child to adult." But just in case he's incorrect, older folks could at least have been isolated, as could those who were younger but unhealthy. Government funds for this purpose would have been tiny in comparison with the trillions it's now paying to stave off bankruptcy resulting from the restricted economy.

The widespread lockdowns may be causing more deaths than the disease itself because of suicide, alcoholism, depression, debts, and medical care too long deferred. Deaths in undeveloped nations due to the slow economies in developed nations probably number in the millions. The lockdowns are criminal.

Prediction: The polls in this month of July 2020 show President Trump losing soundly to Vice President Biden. I nevertheless predict that Donald Trump will be reelected in November 2020. This book will probably go to press before the election. If so, this prediction cannot be purified after the result becomes known. (On October 16, 2020, at my final review of the book, I am even more certain of Trump's victory. The lines of people seeking to attend Mr. Trump's rallies seem endless. The number of people attending some of Mr. Biden's rallies, except for reporters, would hardly fill a phone booth.)

COMPARISON OF LOCKDOWNS

August 24, 2020. In terms of COVID-19 deaths and unemployment rates, Ethan Yang compared states that did not lock down with those whose lockdowns were draconian.[47] The article presents data for all fifty states. I isolate the results for six.

First, the death rates for three benign states: (The number of deaths per 100,000 in the population appear in parentheses): Wyoming (5), Utah (12), and South Dakota (17).

The death rates for three draconian states: New Jersey (179), New York (169), and Massachusetts (128).

The draconian states are more urbanized than the three rural states. With city dwellers pressed together, one would expect their death rates to be higher. But not *that* much higher. The three states that did not lock down may have experienced more immunity, reducing their deaths.

Next, we show the same six states in terms of the increases in the unemployment rates from July 2019 to July 2020:

Wyoming (3.4), Utah (2.0), and South Dakota (3.0).

New Jersey (10.5), New York (12.0), and Massachusetts (13.2).

A stark contrast. Shutting down the economies was ruinous to employment, with no offsetting benefits from the reduction of deaths. Employment in South Dakota remained remarkably good despite the state's significant decline in oil drilling during the period.

The following brief column, drafted for the final chapter, is duplicated here:

Pandemic in a Libertarian Society

If a libertarian society is attacked by a pandemic, the government would do nothing about it. A great deal of advice would be given in the media and on the Internet, some good, some

---

47. AIER, Ethan Yang, *A Closer Look at the States that Stayed Open,* 8/24/20.

bad, but none by government. With no fear of antitrust lawsuits, companies and associations would plan how to meet the crisis. Every citizen would deal with the matter as he or she chose. Widespread immunity would be achieved as quickly as possible.

CHAPTER 5 – HEALTHCARE

JUNE 28, 2017. U.S. HEALTHCARE is a costly mess because nearly every part of it is infested by government. If the federal government would just get out, costs would fall and quality would rise, especially for the poor.

Here's the main cause of the higher costs: When you obtain a health service, an insurance company or the government pays most of the bill, not you. You have little incentive to ask, "What's the cost?" With someone else paying, why bother? Most hospital doctors don't even *know* the costs.

With non-healthcare products, buyers do indeed know the costs. Suppliers are thus in competition with one another, and the competition keeps costs down. If people were aware of their healthcare costs and put suppliers in competition, you could bet the prices would fall.

Imagine going to a supermarket, buying the food you want, and billing an insurance company for 80% of the cost. Forget about hot dogs; only prime steak would do. And why not? You'd have to pay just 20% of the cost. If our food costs were paid mostly by third parties, the total costs would probably double, and their availability would likely fall by half, especially for the poor.

Here now is the Number One change America's healthcare needs: The first several thousand dollars of healthcare costs each year should be paid by the individual receiving the service. Above this amount, every penny would be paid by a low-cost, catastrophic insurance policy, such as most Americans acquired only a few decades ago, before government made its – ha! – improvements.

Let's say you suffer a gash on your arm. Under the current system, off you go to a hospital emergency room. The cost is $2,000, most of which you don't pay. You wait around for hours.

Under the new system, you choose a clinic to patch you up within an hour. You pay $75, a cost you didn't incur before. But the premiums on your new catastrophic insurance policy have declined far more than $75 a year from what they were under the old system. Plus, the hospital's emergency room, now in serious competition with outside clinics, reduces its staff to cut its costs.

Yes, we feel badly about the hospital personnel who are laid off. Some of them might go to work for the new clinics. But the nation's healthcare system should not provide featherbedding for excess medical personnel. The system does indeed serve that purpose now because associations of hospitals, physicians, medical personnel, and insurance companies lobby Congress to retain the current costly system.

Lobbying is legal, but members of Congress should be subject to single terms so they can resist such lobbying and meet the people's needs instead of their own.

The Number Two healthcare change needed: The government should sharply limit the penalties from medical malpractice lawsuits, making it easy for clinics to write legally binding restrictions on liability. With the liability issue settled, low-cost clinics would spring up everywhere.

Under the current, high-cost system, your doctor is afraid of being sued for malpractice. She calls for numerous tests to make sure you're okay. The penalties from tort laws, mostly benefiting the lawyers, should be capped so that at least some of the tests would be considered unnecessary, lowering costs.

Number Three. Insurance companies should be allowed to offer a range of policies, some with high coverage and high premiums, others with low coverage and low premiums.

Let's say you don't feel the need to be kept alive by heroic measures at the end of your life. You would buy a policy that enables you to be kept comfortable while nature takes its course and not given extraordinary and unnatural treatments. Bingo, your premiums would fall significantly, right from the start.

Four. Before giving approval for drugs, the federal government currently tests for two things: whether the drug is safe and whether it works better than the competition or a placebo.

Wait a minute! The government doesn't test *other* products to determine whether they're better than the competition or a placebo. Those matters are decided by buyers. Omitting that second test would cut the cost of prescription drugs.

Five. Why should health insurance premiums be deductible for people who are employed when they're not deductible for individuals who work for themselves? Everyone should be treated the same.

Government interference suppresses innovation. Healthcare is ripe for the kind of efficiencies that have occurred in other industries. Without government involvement, Americans, especially poor Americans, would pay far less for healthcare and enjoy higher quality and greater availability.

CONGRESS COULD SAVE US BILLIONS ON HEALTHCARE

February 25, 2019. Here's why healthcare is so costly:

Hospitals are labor-intensive and therefore have high costs that change little despite the number of patients rising or falling. Decades ago, hospitals developed a special kind of insurance policy whose premiums assured the hospitals regular income and promised policyholders free hospital care in return. Similar policies were later adopted by all healthcare suppliers.[48]

The government and its handmaidens, the insurance companies, thus became third-party payers. Except for small consumer co-payments, they now cover everyone's healthcare costs from the first dollar, creating forest-consuming mounds of paperwork.

With someone else paying, healthcare consumers couldn't care less about the costs. Suppliers don't compete on price, and prices soar.

Hospitals and doctors, in effect, work for the governmental setup that pays them, not for us. They benefit from Americans overpaying for healthcare, and their associations lobby to retain the miserable system.

Congress is the culprit for not resisting the pressure. It should require that policies have substantial deductibles. Consumers would pay for their own healthcare up to the deductible amount and would darn well care about the costs. Many would stop seeing doctors unnecessarily. Suppliers would compete on price, and prices would plummet.

Premiums and administrative costs would also fall because insurance companies would pay nothing until the policyholder's costs for the year exceed the deductible. For many, especially younger people, the insurance companies would pay nothing. The result would be big savings in insurance premiums for everyone, not to mention huge savings on paperwork.

First-dollar payments by third parties are the most important reason the nation's healthcare costs are so high. Spineless Congress is a disgrace for not discarding the wretched system, which would save Americans billions of dollars.

---

48. Imprimis, John Steele Gordon, *A Short History of American Medical Insurance,* September 2018.

PREAUTHORIZATION[49]

Insurance companies increasingly require doctors to seek the insurance company's approval before they administer treatments. The purpose is to cut waste and ensure quality. But preauthorization causes long delays and sometimes deprives patients of the care they need. Plus, it's a royal pain for doctors, causing some of them to quit the business.

Insurance companies get the blame for this, but it's not their fault. The companies can't grab cash out of thin air. They obtain money for healthcare from the government, and the government is under increasing pressure from the public to cut costs.

Here's the basic problem: Except for the silly co-pays, consumers of healthcare don't pay the initial dollars of cost. It is Medicare, Medicaid, or their sidekicks – the insurance companies – that pay. Why should the consumers care what the costs are?

Government is *supposed* to care about costs. But government is the last place anyone should consult about cutting costs. It loves to spend other people's money. It likes to avoid being blamed and is only too pleased that the public thinks insurance companies are the source of the problem.

Neurosurgeon Richard Menger is the lead editor of the academic textbook, "The Business, Policy, and Economics of Neurosurgery." Previously, he ran a neurosurgery clinic in Shreveport, LA, and cites an example from that experience. One of the clinic's patients was crippled by pain in her back and legs and showed the symptoms of compression in her lower spinal nerves. But before they could run an MRI to confirm the diagnosis, they needed approval from the insurance company. For nearly half an hour, they had to argue with the company's non-physician employee while the patient writhed in pain. If the patient wanted surgery, he or she would have needed preauthorization for that as well.

Dr. Menger continues, "Since Louisiana expanded Medicaid in 2016,

49. WSJ, Richard Menger, *The Insurer Will See You Now,* 9/3/18.

the burden of preauthorization on our clinic has become unsustainable, causing our team of doctors to waste countless hours that otherwise could have been spent with the 70-80 patients that need to be seen each week."

The American Medical Association has estimated that preauthorization cost the healthcare system $728 million in 2012 alone, and the problem has since gotten worse. A 2016 survey by the Medical Group Management Association found that 82% of healthcare providers had to contend with increased preauthorization requirements in the preceding year.

Preauthorization makes insurers rather than physicians the primary gatekeepers of care.

THE AMERICANS WITH DISABILITIES ACT[50]

August 20, 2020. The ADA, thirty years old this year, is loaded with fraud. Some people call it "The Attorney's Dream Answered."

The law says anyone is disabled who claims they have significant trouble "standing, lifting, bending, reading, concentrating, or thinking." Whom, pray tell, does this exclude?

Any disabled person acquires a legal right to request accommodations from an employer and others. The federal government and private lawyers stand ready to sue those who fail to accommodate. The government, in fact, sought to achieve progress by maximizing the number of lawsuits. What a ridiculously expensive, lawyer-enriching way to deal with any public issue! Because of the miserable tort industry, lawsuits have proliferated. Progress, not so much.

Hundreds of Florida businesses were hit with ADA lawsuits in 2015 and 2019, demanding compensation because "the pipes in the bathrooms weren't properly wrapped."

Four law firms in 2019 filed more than 100 class actions, charging that retailers are marketing gift cards without Braille versions.

---

50. AIER, James Bovard, *After Thirty Years, Did the Disabilities Act Work?* 7/20/20.

An obese New York hospital ex-employee sued the hospital for $10 million because she was fired after twice falling asleep on her job as an ambulance dispatcher.

A former Chicago policeman sought $75,000 in damages because he was fired after driving drunk, hitting and badly injuring a pedestrian, and leaving the scene of the accident. This violated the ADA, he maintained, because he had Post-Traumatic Stress Disorder.

If government stopped trying to care for the disabled, the job would be performed better and more honestly by the private sector, some for profit and some not. Call it "People Caring for People."

PRIVATIZE THE VETERANS ADMINISTRATION

May 20, 2019. You want socialism? You got it already. It's called the VA.

The entire defense department, including all the military services, stands at 738,000 employees. The postal service has 634,000 employees. The Veterans Administration comes in third, with 373,000 employees, almost twice that of any other non-military agency.[51]

Since 2001, the VA's budget has grown almost five times, with numerous management changes. Yet the agency has been a continual source of negligence, falsified records, and mismanagement.

Prior to joining the military, people had higher levels of education, less illness, less criminality, and less family decay than their non-military peers. But after getting out, veterans have suffered higher rates of substance abuse, suicide, and intentional unemployment. What a turnaround! Even though few veterans since 2011 have experienced combat, they're hurting anyway. Yes, they're hurting from their dependence on a miserable government agency.[52]

51. I obtained these employee numbers from the Web.
52. Where all this information came from I no longer remember. I certainly didn't make it up. A friend, a retired and very competent nurse practitioner, has read a number of my columns. The only comment she made about all of them was, "You sure are right about the VA."

Veterans should instead use healthcare services of the private economy, paid by government insurance policies, with deductibles paid first by the veterans.

The VA itself should be terminated, with its facilities sold to the highest bidders. Don't expect high prices, however, because the nation already has too many hospitals. Instead of each hospital in a locality specializing in certain capabilities, almost every hospital in every locality strives to offer a full array of capabilities. This is one of the many ways the federal government, directly and indirectly, has made a mess of American healthcare.

The VA, owned and operated by the government, is the worst of it.

MEDICAL SCHOOLS HAVE BECOME POLITICIZED

November 4, 2019. In a Wall Street Journal editorial,[53] Dr. Stanley Goldfarb, former associate dean of curriculum at the University of Pennsylvania's Perelman School of Medicine, regretted that American medical schools are placing less emphasis on teaching the fundamentals of diseases and the interpretation of symptoms. Without objecting to doctors having their own political views, Dr. Goldfarb deplored that medical schools now focus on social justice, with sociology and social work the driving forces to achieve it. The schools emphasize climate change, gun control, social inequities, cultural diversity, and elimination of bias. Medical school bureaucracies have become bloated, with many key administrative positions held by those who hold Masters of Education.

After Dr. Goldfarb's column appeared, the WSJ disclosed that the dean and vice dean of the Penn Medical School wrote to students and faculty this shining example of political correctness:[54]

"Please know that the views expressed by Dr. Goldfarb in his col-

53. WSJ, Stanley Goldfarb, *Take Two Aspirin and Call Me by My Pronouns,* 9/12/19.
54. WSJ Editorial Board, *Corrupting Medical Education,* 9/15/19.

umn reflect his personal opinions and do not reflect the values of the Perelman School of Medicine. We deeply value inclusion and diversity as fundamental to effective healthcare delivery, creativity, discovery, and life-long learning. We are committed to ensuring a rigorous and comprehensive medical education that includes examination of the many social and cultural issues that influence health, from violence within communities to changes in the environment around us."

Yes, understanding about community violence and world environmental issues are essential in learning how to treat human illnesses. Well, this is true according to the dean and vice dean of the Penn Medical School anyway.

But if you're sick but don't want a lecture on diversity or climate change, avoid graduates of that school.

The root cause of the politicization of medical schools? Federal funding. Ideas flow from whence the money comes.

DISABILITY INSURANCE[55]

Social Security's Disability Insurance program offers payments to those who become disabled before retiring. Financed by payroll taxes, the program paid $144 billion in 2018.

The number of recipients was 3 million in the early 1980s. Congress then relaxed the requirements. Surprise, surprise, the number grew to 8.5 million people by 2018.

To demonstrate an inability to work, a worker can cite not just a major debilitating condition, but also smaller ailments, such as back pain. If disability is denied, the applicant can appeal the decision up to four times. Overwhelmed with appeals, administrative officials simply give in and award benefits to excess.

The disability program is highly susceptible to fraud. Each year, only

---

55. WSJ Editorial, *About That "Gutting the Safety Net,"* 5/30/17.

about 1% of beneficiaries return to work. Most benefits are terminated when the recipient dies or transfers to a retiree program. One study estimated that about half of the applicants age 30 to 44 would find a job again if their application for disability were denied.

In some cases, the disability income, plus healthcare benefits, food stamps, and other benefits rival the person's potential working income. Remaining on welfare becomes the reasonable choice.

Unfortunately, disability insurance has been expanded to cover mental health issues. Mental health professionals maintain that a job and social connections are more likely to alleviate anxiety and depression than remaining on welfare.

America's government disability insurance program should be terminated. Caring people in the private sector, raising money from the prosperous, would deal with the issue fairly but at far less cost.

PRE-EXISTING CONDITIONS

Let's say you own a house with no fire insurance. One night, the house burns to the ground. The next day, you buy a fire insurance policy that has a pre-existing condition: The house no longer exists. The insurance company has accumulated no premiums from you, but accepting your policy would require the company to buy you a new house. This isn't insurance; it's welfare.

Now let's say you have a medical condition that requires ongoing care. You buy a medical insurance policy. The insurance company has accumulated no premiums regarding your condition. If it's required to accept the pre-condition, it must raise the premiums of all of its policyholders to cover the cost.

Politicians observe that the benefit to you is obvious and substantial, while the extra premium costs spread among all the other policyholders are hidden and small. They therefore require the insurance company to accept the pre-existing health condition.

Multiply this government requirement by thousands of others that incur costs that are hidden and small to cover the costs of people not expected to cover their own costs. All those hidden costs add up, especially since an army of bureaucrats is hired for administration.

And people wonder why the cost of living is so arduous.

CHAPTER 6 – THE ENVIRONMENT

The following column was written with the help and advice of prominent climatologist Patrick J. Michaels, which I appreciate very much. I suggested he be a co-author and try to place the piece with the Wall Street Journal, where I had seen his columns before. No, he had recently been turned down by the Journal and didn't want to try again so soon. I suggested that he even be the sole author to give the ideas exposure. No, he had recently made a discovery and didn't want anything to go out under his name that did not include it. He described the discovery to me in scientific language I didn't fully understand, but I understood enough of it to recognize that it did not invalidate this column.

GLOBAL WARMING: NOT A DANGER

JANUARY 16, 2018. IT'S BEEN cold. No doubt you've noticed.

The greenhouse effect of carbon dioxide (CO_2) in the atmosphere may cause modest warming, but more important is the sun's emissions of energy. These emissions correlate with the number of sunspots. During the last half-century, the number of sunspots has trended downward, which may foreshadow unusually cold weather for a considerable time.

Global warming proponents have consistently exaggerated their warming predictions. They base their work on computer models, which are guesses, not scientific fact. Computer models can readily be manipulated to show what the operators want them to show.

Most of the personal income of scientists comes directly or indirectly from the federal government. It's no surprise that some scientists have become less concerned with the truth and more concerned with toeing the government line.

Here are the approximate warm and cold periods during the last two millennia:

- The earth's temperature warmed from 200 BC to 400 AD. This is referred to as the Roman Climate Optimum.

- It cooled during the Dark Ages from 400 to 900.

- It warmed from 900 to 1300 – the Medieval Warming Period. Around the year 1000, not a single SUV could be found, but the world was nevertheless warmer than it is now.

- The world cooled from 1300 to 1860 – the Mini-Ice Age. The period from 1645 to 1715, referred to as the Maunder Minimum, was especially cold. There were no sunspots during those years.

- The earth warmed from 1860 to 1940.

- From 1940 to 1975, it cooled. Fossil fuel emissions during World War II and the three decades that followed brought large percentage increases in atmospheric CO2. Despite this spurt, the earth cooled.

- Warming occurred from 1975 to 1998.

Professor Michael Mann's renowned "hockey stick" graph omits the medieval warming period from 900 to 1300 and the Mini-Ice Age from 1300 to 1860. His graph shows world temperatures remaining flat until about 1850, then roaring upward, making the current warming seem like an anomaly.

Much has been made of the diminishment of Arctic ice. But while this was occurring, the ice surrounding the Antarctic was the widest in recorded history due, perhaps, to a wobbling of the earth's axis. After the *March of the Penguins* movie was seen, hundreds of thousands of penguin chicks died because the parents were unable to cross the widened ice sheet in time to feed them.

Fears of rising ocean levels are exaggerated. Glaciers have been melting and oceans rising for more than 12,000 years. Since 1860, the ocean has risen at about 3 millimeters a year, without gaining speed in recent years. At this rate, an increase of even one meter would take more than three centuries.

When wheat, rice, soybeans, cotton, and other widely used plants evolved more than 65 million years ago, atmospheric CO2 was at least 3,000 parts per million, far above today's 400 ppm. Plant life flourished.

Oh yes, the polar bears are flourishing.

Global warming proponents acknowledge that a significant reduction of fossil fuels would reduce the earth's temperature a century from now by less than year-to-year fluctuations. They recommend the reductions anyway, even though the resulting shortage of food could cause millions of poor people in the world to starve.

From 1940 to 1975, the earth cooled. Global warming proponents predicted we were doomed from the cold. Fossil fuels were the cause. Bigger and more intrusive government to force the reduction of atmospheric CO2 was the solution.

From 1975 to 1998, the earth warmed. The proponents predicted we were doomed from the heat. Fossil fuels were the cause. Bigger and more intrusive government was the solution.

The proponents now tout anecdotal evidence that weather changes have been more extreme than usual. We're doomed. Fossil fuels are the cause. Bigger and more intrusive government is the solution.

Fossil fuels may cause luke-warming, but the notion that fossil fuels are putting mankind in danger is way overblown. The world now spends $1 billion a day to cut fossil fuel usage. It's an outrageous waste.

DISASTROUS FOREST FIRES LOOM[56]

January 28, 2019. The forest fire around Paradise, CA, incinerated 153,000 acres. But California charcoal deposits reveal that prehistoric wildfires destroyed between 4.5 and 11.9 million acres every year. When Juan Cabrillo anchored in San Pedro Bay in October 1542, he named it the "Bay of Smoke."

An unattended forest grows until it's choked with kindling. After a big burn in 1910, the U.S. Forest Service began managing its forests scientifically. Foresters designated surplus trees, and loggers who'd won at auctions removed them.

This didn't suit the environmentalists. Why? It's hard to know. Maybe they feel it's wrong for mankind to dominate the environment in any way. Perhaps they think we should all return to hunting and fishing, like early man, outrunning forest fires whenever possible. But they certainly don't want to miss their lattes and New York Times on Sunday mornings.

Anyway, the environmentalists pressured Congress in the 1970s to slow down the culling of trees. Timber harvesting declined sharply, and forest fires increased.

Environmentalists blamed the fires on global warming, of course. But it is primarily the forests owned by the government that have burned, not the ones privately owned and scientifically managed. U.S. Representative Tom McClintock, of California, wrote, "It's clever of the climate to decimate only the lands hamstrung by environmental laws."

Forest fires flood the atmosphere with CO_2. Good forest management, in contrast, confines the carbon inside living trees or in the lumber from harvested trees.

---

56. WSJ, Tom McClintock, *Only Good Management Can Prevent Forest Fires,* 12/18/18.

In its arrogance, know-it-all Congress directs the Forest Service how many trees it must cull each year. Too many, and the Service clear-cuts, as it has done in the past. Too few, as Congress has called for recently, and the danger of fire grows.

The danger of forest fires is indeed growing. A typical acre in the Sierra can support about 80 mature trees. The current density is more than 300 trees.

Nature will eventually take its course. Fire disasters loom.

CLEARING THE AMAZON RAINFOREST

A New York Times article[57] lamented that Brazil's "far-right" President Bolsonoro had removed restrictions that had restricted people from clearing the Amazon rainforest. The article lamented that the rainforest had lost more than 1,330 square miles of forest during the seven months after Mr. Bolsonoro took office. "Vast stretches of the rainforest can be torn down," "We're facing the risk of runaway deforestation," opined the article.

Really? Let's see: The Amazon rainforest occupies 2.124 million square miles. If the clearing continues at the above pace, 1,330 square miles in seven months, it would take 932 years to clear the entire forest (2.124 million/1,330 x 7/12).

Way to capture the full, unbiased story, NYT. Keep printing all the news that's fit for liberals to read.

Poor countries are deforesting. But as people move from rural areas to cities, rich countries are reforesting. Since 1982, the U.S. has left to nature areas totaling that of the state of Washington.

According to an article from AIER,[58] nations whose per capita GDP is below $7,800 are generally losing their forest stock. Nations whose per

57. NY Times, Leticia Casado and Ernesto Londono, *Under Brazil's Far-Right Leader, Amazon Protections Slashed and Forests Fall*, 7/28/19.
58. AIER, Joakim Book, *Brazilians Should Keep Slashing Their Rainforest*, 3/17/20.

capita GDP is above $7,800 are gaining it.

British science writer Matt Ridley commented that populations of wolves in rich countries are increasing. Populations of tigers in middle-income countries are holding steady, and populations of lions in poor countries are falling. The more prosperous the citizens, the more concerned they are about the environment.

President Bolsonoro wants the Amazon people to use portions of the rainforest to get rich. After that, they can let the forest regrow.

Seems reasonable to me.

GLOBAL WARMING ISN'T ALL BAD

Climate change is mainly a pretext for liberals to expand government control, redistribute wealth, and empower elites.

Atmospheric CO_2 is wonderful for plant life. Since 1982, the earth's green foliage has expanded by an area twice the size of the continental U.S., providing food for millions.

The increases in temperature predicted by global warming models have consistently been too high. They've predicted that the pace of ocean rising would quicken. It has not.

Fossil fuel emissions during World War II and the three decades that followed brought large percentage increases in atmospheric CO_2. Despite this spurt from 1940 to 1975, the earth cooled. I know of no global warming proponent who's been able to explain why.

Technologies exist to capture ample sunlight with solar collectors in space and beam the energy to earth. Other CO_2-saving technologies include nuclear power and harnessing the ocean's wave motion.

Free market capitalism would bring these developments. Global warming acolytes don't cotton to free market capitalism. They prefer to reorganize society, supposedly to spread the wealth more equally. But the changes they favor would actually make everyone equally *poor*, with the people holding the political power and their cronies the most equal of all.

Only one computer model has accurately estimated warming trends in the bulk atmosphere over the past 40 years. It's Russian, with the charming name of INM-CM5. According to the 10/2/17 issue of *Science Matters*, when that model is run with a realistic scenario in which gas increasingly displaces coal as an electricity fuel, the world meets the Paris climate treaty's warming limit without using force.

Sorry, the liberals aren't interested. They enjoy those international confabs. The food is scrumptious.

COLD WEATHER MAY DRAW NEAR

The earth could suffer a period of significant cold weather.

Bjorn Lomborg, author and former director of the Danish government's Environmental Assessment Institute, wrote this about carbon dioxide: "It's almost magical thinking to suppose that a gas consisting of only four-hundredths of one percent of the atmosphere would have more influence on the earth's temperature than the enormous amounts of energy received from the sun."

By far, the greatest influence on the earth's temperature is the sun's energy. When this falls, the earth becomes colder. The cooling of the sun is preceded or accompanied by a reduction of sunspots.

From 1645 to 1715, the earth was very cold. This period was named the "Maunder Minimum," after Northern Irish astronomer Annie Maunder. During those 70 years, no sunspots could be seen, even though numerous scientists were looking for them with telescopes (which Galileo had invented in 1609). It was the longest known period of no sunspots.

From 1840 to 1900, the number of sunspots declined significantly. Thereafter, from 1905 to 1912, the earth's temperatures became unusually cold.

From 1950 to the present, sunspots have again declined. There seems to be a race between cold weather signaled by the declining sunspots and warmer weather from increased levels of CO_2. Which will prevail, no one knows.

But if natural gas, atomic power, and newly developing sources of energy become widely used, the advance of CO_2 will be reversed. The sun's cooling effect, signaled by the declining sunspots, might then prevail, causing significant cold weather.

Technology hasn't found a way to control the sun. (If technology continues to advance, I wouldn't be surprised if this will be achieved within a couple of hundred years).

GLOBAL COOLING

The earth's outer atmosphere receives about 5% more energy from the sun in one hour than mankind uses in an entire year.

Entrepreneurs could set up big solar collectors in space, beam the energy to earth by microwave, and bingo, everyone on earth would have energy that is nearly free. The technology exists.

Industry would no longer be ejecting extra CO_2 into the atmosphere. Planes that wandered into forbidden space containing the microwave would probably be incinerated, but big planes carrying passengers would rarely be so careless. The oil, coal, and natural gas industries would have a little something to say about capturing our energy needs from space because most of them would lose their jobs. Liberals would squawk because they'd be deprived of refashioning society by force. But the great bulk of mankind would benefit hugely.

For many decades, the eleven-year sun cycle and the number of sun spots has been diminishing. The sun is emitting less energy than usual, foretelling several decades of very cold weather, possibly such as occurred during the Maunder Minimum of 1645 to 1715.

But because of the greenhouse effect of the extra atmospheric carbon dioxide produced by man, the earth has not been getting colder. A tug of war has existed. Less energy is being emitted from the sun. But more energy is being imprisoned in the atmosphere because of the extra CO_2. So far, the CO_2 is winning.

If solar collectors in space provide us with the energy we need, however, the greenhouse effect will no longer operate because the use of fossil fuels would decline a great deal. Several decades of very cold weather would likely ensue.

MARINE STEWARDSHIP COUNCIL[59]

The Marine Stewardship Council (MSC), created by environmentalists and businesses, is a wonderful example of people in the private sector banding together to accomplish by free choice and free markets what government has accomplished badly by force.

The MSC has developed scientific standards to measure fisheries for the following:

- They may not deplete fish populations,

- They must minimize bycatch (mortality of non-target marine animals), and

- They must show respect for the environmental integrity of the bodies of water they use.

The council has offices worldwide that certify seafood from ocean to plate. Certified products are clearly labeled. They're traceable back to their sustainable source and kept separate from non-certified products.

Fisheries are certified every five years and may use the certification in marketing their products. But unlike its competitors, MSC also subjects certified fisheries to surveillance audits every year. If any of the 28

59. AIER, Jeffery A. Tucker, "Sustainable Fish": Real or Marketing Ploy? 2020.

performance indicators fall below a certain score, the certification may be suspended. If standards are not met by the end of the five years, the fishery may not recertify.

The council is funded by dues and payments for audits, currently ranging from $15,000 to $100,000.

The council is also audited by an independent auditor of fisheries to prevent any possible corruption or payoffs by the council itself. It is also policed by other environmental groups. Greenpeace, for example, has disputed some of the council's judgments. The opinions were hashed out and compromises arrived at.

When a fishery loses its MSC designation, grocery stores who care, such as Whole Foods and many other stores, stop buying from it. No legislation, no government planning, and no coercion are involved.

Fifteen percent of the world's seafood is MSC-certified and sold from 38,000 sites. This is a start; it's an enormous industry, and there are other similar organizations. You may read more about the council at msc.org.

Interested private parties can improve the environment successfully without government involvement.

Chapter 7 – Racism

Little Remains of America's Racism[60]

AFTER A COLUMN OF MINE in the Concord Monitor pointed out that racism is no longer an important factor in American life, George countered, "A black person from a central city is about three times more likely to be rejected for a mortgage than his white counterpart. That's racism."

No it isn't. If both applicants have similar employment, income, and family situations, and neither one has a police record, you can bet that the bank officer would provide mortgages to both parties, not only because she'd want to, but also because the liberal press is prone to label people racist at the drop of a hat. The loan officer might well be black herself.

George's letter continued, "Central city blacks are likely to be behind in terms of employment, income, family situations, and police records. Surely this is evidence of racism."

Not so. By far, the most important cause of the disparity between whites and blacks is government policies that are not intended to hurt the poor but, in the long run, hurt them anyway. I count 38 such policies.

Advertisements are telling. Until 1960, when America was indeed racist, blacks were usually shown in ads as subservient to whites. Now,

---

60. Letter to the Concord Monitor, *Barriers exist, even the ones you can't see*, 12/1/17. George's last name is of course withheld.

television ads show blacks as equals.

Liberals seem unaware of how much America has changed. They don't welcome such change because they endeavor to attain power by encouraging the belief that the nation is racist.

AMERICAN RACISM NO LONGER NEEDS GOVERNMENT'S ATTENTION

September 23, 2019. American racism is much diminished.

Black experience in America is far from ideal, of course. Family instability and fatherlessness in black communities is a big problem. Big city, unionized schools provide miserable education. The war on drugs puts potential black entrepreneurs in jail, cutting short otherwise productive careers. And numerous government policies, including minimum wages, government lotteries, and occupational licensing, make life more costly for the poor of all colors.

Back in the 1950s, America truly was racist. Today, a small minority remains racist, but America as a whole is not. Here is evidence:

- The nation twice elected a black president. States with big pluralities of whites, like New Hampshire, voted for Obama both times.

- In the 1950s, movies portrayed blacks as passive and deferential. Now, blacks play forceful leading roles.

- Advertisers want ads to result in maximum sales of the products being advertised. They try to affect people emotionally as well as intellectually. In the 1950s, blacks seldom appeared in ads because racist whites were unwilling to be advised by blacks about how to spend their money. Now, no longer racist, whites willingly follow the lead of assertive blacks advising them what products they should buy.

- Michelle Obama and Oprah Winfrey are among America's most admired women. Until recently, Bill Cosby was considered the nation's most admired man. Never would such approbations have occurred in the 1950s.

When a social or economic problem is solved, it should no longer attract government's attention. But this could cause government workers to lose their jobs, a prospect that lacks appeal for them. It is in their interest that government continue to proclaim racism as a major problem. It is not. American racism no longer requires government's attention.

AMERICAN RACISM: PERPETUATED BY GOVERNMENT

There's racism in America, all right – on the part of government and its sidekicks, the unions:

- Government-supported teachers' unions care greatly about teachers' pay and the continued employment of poor teachers. They care far less about the quality of education, especially for blacks in central cities.

- Minimum wage laws cause unemployment among those whose value to an employer is less than the minimum wage. The laws are a key reason why young black males (at least until the reduction of income tax rates in 2018) have suffered an unemployment rate of approximately 50%. It is not racist for an employer to refuse to hire someone whose hourly value is less than the minimum wage. It's the laws themselves that are racist.

- Indirectly, the war on drugs is racist. Blacks who engage in the illegal drug business are, in effect, entrepreneurs. It's tragic that such people end up in jail instead of benefiting society, as they probably would without drug criminalization. If children of the elite were being sent to jail in great numbers for drug violations, the war on drugs would quickly be terminated.

- The Federal Reserve Bank helps the rich and hurts the poor by setting price controls on interest rates. With the rates low, creditors lend to the rich and big businesses, confident of repayment. But the creditors hesitate to lend to poor and small businesses for fear of default. Small businesses, usually the biggest source of new jobs, are therefore forced to reduce their hiring.

- The FTC forces up the prices of sugar, citrus, and other products. The U.S. price of sugar, in fact, is significantly higher than the world price. The poor pay more, while the relatively few U.S. sugar producers and citrus growers benefit greatly.

- The Davis-Bacon Act, enacted more than 80 years ago, artificially inflates the wages of construction workers and employs an army of bureaucrats to enforce its measures.[61] Contractors are required to pay construction workers "local prevailing wages" on all federally funded jobs. A backhoe operator in New York State, including benefits, currently earns $99.39 an hour. (This column was probably written in 2019.) Citizens in New York pay high tolls for using such facilities.

- An intent of the Davis-Bacon Act back during the Great Depression was to prevent non-unionized blacks from competing for scarce jobs with unionized whites. Minorities continue to be underrepresented in unionized skilled trades. In 2009, the Obama administration expanded the coverage of Davis-Bacon, making construction projects all the more expensive and racist. Rewarding unions for their campaign contributions, it seems, had a higher priority.

- Welfare keeps the poor down by generating dependency and

61. WSJ, Philip Mark Plotch, *Bringing Home the Davis-Bacon,* 12/1/16.

destroying individual initiative. It also terminates when a job is found. If a minimum wage job is found, the modest extra income from the job, over and above the income lost from welfare, induces the person to remain on welfare. Private parties that take the place of government welfare would be aware of such niceties and do everything possible to enable people to obtain jobs.

- As government has grown, the gap between rich and poor has become wider. Rich people and big businesses provide substantial funds to help reelect legislators, receiving benefits in return. This is called crony capitalism, in which the poor are unable to engage. For more than a decade, the real income of America's lower economic groups has remained about level, while the rich have thrived. Liberals *say* they want to help the poor, but they fail to notice that their policies have the opposite effect.

- Unions raise the income of the few union members to unnatural levels (meaning not set by a free market according to the supply and demand of labor). But this causes higher prices for everyone else. Without the laws and regulations that support unions, they would be far less effective in raising labor costs. Nor could they afford to make such large campaign contributions to liberal members of Congress.

- (Written in June, 2020 and added here.) George Floyd was not killed because of racism. He was killed because of a union. The policeman who murdered Floyd has been accused more than a dozen times of using excessive force. Every time, the police union has jumped to his defense to save his job. Even now, the union is gearing up with defense lawyers to preserve his job once again.

Unions could not survive in their present detrimental form without federal laws that support them. Union laws do great damage to America.

Disrespecting the Anthem

The rich have thrived partly because of billions of crony government dollars that aid them. Despite promises to help the poor, big government policies have hurt them instead. After inflation, low-income people in the last 20 years, based on their earned income, have become poorer.

Not realizing that liberalism is to blame, prosperous liberals have adopted the view that America is racist, sexist, homophobic, and militaristic. But these are bigotries of old. Black commentator Shelby Steele of Stanford University's Hoover Institution, writes, "Bigotry exists, but it is far down on the list of problems that minorities now face."[62]

Apparently, the millionaire football players disrespecting the nation's anthem seem unaware of how much America has changed. The comradery between white and black football players is itself evidence that racism no longer remains an important factor.

No, the primary source of racism is big government liberalism.

---

62. WSJ, Shelby Steele, *The Exhaustion of American Liberalism*, 3/6/17.

CHAPTER 8 – LIBERALISM

THE ESSENCE OF MODERN LIBERALISM

NOVEMBER 2, 2020. THE ACTIVISTS and leaders of modern liberalism are generally unhappy. They compensate for their lack of self-assurance by presuming they are superior to others. Liberals believe it is they who are moral; the rest of America is "deplorable." They believe that many political groups, being victims, are not self-reliant and must be taken care of by liberals. Markets must be rendered unfree by heavy regulation. Liberals want to restructure the entire society. The nation's laws are whatever the liberals say they are at any one moment. The Constitution can be disregarded.

The media and social media have superior insight too. This enables them to exclude bad news about Democrats and exclude good news about Republicans.

Even after a black was twice elected president, liberals promoted "systematic racism." Its purpose is to make people feel guilty, rendering them susceptible to liberal views. Systematic racism is nonsense. Isolated racism is more like it.

Energy affects every aspect of our lives. By highlighting global warming, liberals endeavor to control our lives in every possible way. They have no interest in technologies that would halt emissions of atmospheric CO2. Their objective is to gain political control.

Conservatives cannot discuss these matters with liberals. Liberals are unable to discuss; they can only lecture about public affairs. Conservatives cannot find common ground with a group that wants conservatives to stop saying or writing anything that makes liberals feel uncomfortable.

Federal funding of colleges and universities has enabled the development of most of these absurd notions, which are poisoning the minds of young Americans.

Conservatives must defeat liberals over and over in elections, eventually rendering them irrelevant.

HOW LIBERALS DISCUSS POLITICS

May 27, 2017. In a recent conversation with a friend, I mentioned that I'd written a newspaper column stating that the 2008 Credit Crisis had been caused by wretched federal government policies. The discussion immediately became unpleasant. (The next time we saw each other, we remained friends). This column is based on that conversation, although I have had other similar discussions.

Liberals believe that most social and economic problems should be solved by government laws and regulations. Libertarians, like me, believe that government should be sharply limited.

Liberals often respond to opposing views in the following ways:

- They interrupt. Liberals seem to want to prevent people with opposing views from talking.

- They turn political discussion into an argument, accompanied by a rise in volume and intensity of voice.

- They mischaracterize opposing statements. After I said the federal government caused the 2008 Credit Crisis, my friend responded, "What? You don't want *any* government?" There's a big difference between faulty government policies and no government at all.

- They try to change the subject. The mischaracterization cited above also moved the discussion away from the 2008 Credit Crisis.

Liberals promise that government will solve economic and social problems and help the poor. But they fail to notice that, in the long run, big government has neither solved the problems nor prevented the gap between rich and poor from widening. The promises and good intentions make liberals feel like good people. Their self-image is closely tied to their intentions, not to reality.

Liberals are prone to blame problems on the character, bad intentions, and greed of business people. I haven't heard them give other reasons in support of their views. They may not have other reasons.

American liberalism hasn't reached an extreme yet, but it may still do so. In the long run, solving social and economic problems by laws and regulations makes the problems worse. Liberals are then inclined to pile on more government, causing yet more problems. The downhill slide could eventually result in conditions like those of Venezuela.

(The above was written in July 2017. At the final review of this book in October 2020, the destruction wrought by Black Lives Matter and other such groups in several U.S. cities indicates that American liberalism is indeed reaching an extreme.)

How should the conversation with my liberal friend have proceeded? After I said the federal government caused the 2008 Credit Crisis, the liberal might have responded, "Why do you say that?" Then it would have been appropriate to just listen. If I proved to be uninformed, my friend could gently move the conversation away from politics. But if I proved to be informed, wouldn't it be appropriate to listen and learn?

Okay, let's see if I can measure up to this high standard myself.

LIBERAL MEDIA'S IMAGINARY WORLD

May 31, 2017. In response to a column of mine, a Concord Monitor reader wrote, "The Republicans have always represented the interests of the one percent, the most conservative billionaires."

My response was as follows: "Let's see: Of the wealthiest Americans listed in the Forbes 400, the top six are Democrats. Then comes two Republicans, and the last two are Democrats. All Republicans, eh?"

The reader lives in the imaginary world painted by the liberal media.

MASS MURDER: PARTLY ENABLED BY LIBERALISM?

October 12, 2017. During the 2012 election, the Obama campaign launched a cartoon ad called "The Life of Julia," showing the life of a fictional woman from ages 3 to 67. Julia had a child, but the ad made no mention of the child's father, Julia's family, or her church. Her life was defined by interactions with government programs that supposedly care for people from cradle to grave.

Liberals support this unrealistic vision of society. They combine it with grievances about victimhood. Except for prosperous white Protestant males, everyone is a victim of something.

Victims are told there's no use taking responsibility for your own life. You can't win. Leave it to government to make things right.

Many people believe these unfulfillable promises, especially in big cities and on the East and West coasts. At universities, grievance is taught big time.

For the mentally unstable, victimhood and grievance have special appeal. For a few people, feelings of hopelessness and revenge induce them to commit mass murder.

As liberalism has advanced, mass murder has become more common. (I have not checked out that statement; it may be a stretch.) But for sure, gun control won't help. I believe removing liberals from office would indeed help.

FORGET CONSENSUS

November 16, 2016. In a letter to the Concord Monitor, the authors cite 31 problems affecting America and conclude, "With votes counted from the November election, consensus needs to be our goal. Everyone needs a place at the table."

Nonsense! For most of the past 115 years, since Teddy Roosevelt, big government liberals have generally been on the ascendancy. By my count, all but 3 of the 31 problems cited in the letter have been caused by the negative long-term consequences of big government policies enacted by liberals.

Small-government Republicans should *not* consult with liberals any more than they have to. Participation by liberals will only lead to more problems. Liberals seldom give in. Do not give in to them. Let voters decide when liberals should be removed from office. If the voters can't decide, let the squabbling continue without resolution. No legislation beats bad legislation.

Liberals, by the way, include not only Democrats, but also Republicans-in-Name-Only. These RINOs should be voted out of office along with Democrats. Fortunately, all such removals began with the Tea Party ten years ago.

Never mind consensus. America's Second Revolution must continue with all deliberate speed.

LIBERALISM IS DYING[63]

October 8, 2018. In a recent Wall Street Journal column, Shelby Steele, black senior fellow at Stanford University's Hoover Institution, said the hatred displayed by the American left signifies that liberalism and the Democratic Party are dying.

In the 1960s, America accepted that slavery and segregation were, as Mr. Steele put it, "profound moral failings." The left took charge of America's moral legitimacy and gained significant political power. This led to the greatest array of government social programs the world has ever seen.

A white-on-black shooting four years ago in Ferguson, MO, resulted in a lengthy media blitz. But thousands of black-on-black shootings in Chicago during those same four years gained little notice. Why? Because the left gains power by fighting white evil, not black despair.

The diminishment of racism threatens the left's power. Unlike the demonstrations of the 1960s, when people donned their Sunday best for marching, today's liberal demonstrations are marked by intolerance, anger, and anti-Americanism. Some liberal demonstrations are marked by incoherence, bizarre sexuality, violence, and vulgarity. Liberals seem to be grasping at straws.

(So much for Mr. Steele. This is me, now.) Some blacks remain poor, of course. But they're not poor because they're black. They're poor because innumerable government programs brought by liberals have widened the gap between rich and poor. For American poor of all colors, laws and regulations have made life more difficult and more costly. The multitude of these government social programs should be reversed. This will narrow the wealth gap and enable the poor of all colors to thrive.

---

63. WSJ, Shelby Steele, *Why the Left is Consumed with Hate*, 9/24/18.

THE NEWS ISN'T NEWS: IT'S POLITICS

Friend Barbara is disgusted with the current political conflicts.

Who can blame you, Barbara? Unfortunately, many activist crowds of recent years have been paid by George Soros and other wealthy liberals. IRS information reveals that Ana Maria Archila, who cornered Senator Flake in a Senate elevator, was paid more than $175,000 as co-executive director of the Center for Popular Democracy, one of numerous Soros-funded organizations.[64] The media doesn't want you to know about this.

Most major television networks are not in the news business; they're in politics. They strive to persuade their viewers to vote Democrat by omitting bad news about Democrats and omitting good news about Republicans. After showing Dr. Christine Ford accusing Brett Kavanaugh of sexual abuse, for example, the networks failed to reveal her inability to remember numerous details about the event in question. The networks have shown plenty of bad news about President Trump, but they've made light of his reversal of government regulations that kept employment and the economy down.

Government is the only part of society that's permitted to exercise force. Used to excess, force foments force, violence begets violence. As a result, conflict eventually permeates society.

For more than a century, the federal government has grown in size and power in an effort to impose the public's well-being by force. By 2010, many Americans realized that society is not improved by widespread government coercion. From 2010 to 2018, twelve hundred Democrats at all levels were voted out of office. The reduction of government will continue, one hopes, narrowing the gap between rich and poor.

Bernie Sanders has maintained that his socialism isn't authoritarian; it's democratic. People have the right to control their own lives, he says.

That's doubtful, Bernie. Your democracy will take place at the ballot

---

64. WSJ, Asra Q. Nomani, *George Soros's March on Washington,* 10/8/18.

box, yes, but it won't prevail thereafter. You want to increase the number of laws and regulations, making even more use of force than is used now. People can control their own lives until they run up against one of your requirements. Under your leadership, this would occur remarkably quickly. Then, either they do it your way or they're fined or go to jail. Of course, they can always persuade the government to change its rules, but this usually requires considerable expertise, time, and money – attributes generally not available to the poor.

INCOME INEQUALITY IS EXAGGERATED

March 23, 2020. In 2017, according to the Census Bureau, the average household in the bottom-fifth of earned income earned $4,908. The average household in the top-fifth earned $295,904, sixty times greater. Some people cite this when urging the government to do more to address the imbalance.

It's disgraceful for the Census Bureau to put out such misleading figures. The average bottom-fifth household actually had net income of $50,901, not $4,908, after accounting for substantial government welfare, gifts from charitable and family sources, and modest taxes paid.

The average top-fifth household, had net income of $194,906, not $295,904, after accounting for substantial taxes paid.

The $194,906 of the top echelon is only 3.8 times greater than the $50,902 of the bottom, not sixty times.[65] The Census Department bends the truth to encourage you to vote for ever bigger government.

Liberals will say that even a difference of 3.8 times is too great a gap.

No, it isn't. People have different talents and capabilities. But America should strive for a difference of 3.8 times *without* the welfare to the poor and taxes of the rich. This would be impossible without a much smaller government.

---

65. WSJ, Phil Gramm & John F. Early, *The Truth about Income Inequality,* 11/4/19.

The top one-percenters are extremely wealthy, of course. But most of them have made significant contributions. When Microsoft founder Bill Gates retired in 2008, he was worth about $50 billion. This was probably a tiny fraction of the contributions Microsoft made to the world's GDP just in that year, never mind other years.

Chapter 9 – Presidents

This was my first column, published by the Union Leader, of Manchester NH, on November 12, 2016.

Trump's Election is the Beginning of a Bloodless Revolution

In last week's election, the people were up against an out-of-control government. The people won. It's the beginning of a bloodless revolution – just the beginning, of course.

Government officials, addicted to excercising power, will fight tooth and nail to prevent slimming down. It'll take years. But Donald Trump is a fighter, which is just what we need. Here are policies he favors:

Strengthen the military. This isn't slimming, of course, but President Obama has starved the U.S. military for funds. Manpower levels are too low. Mechanics must cannibalize fighter planes for parts to keep the others flying. Mr. Obama has frequently threatened "serious consequences" if a foreign nation does something, only to back off. Mr. Trump will probably draw fewer lines in the sand, but stand behind the lines he draws.

Repeal Obamacare. This disastrous law should not be replaced by another government program. Government should just get out of the healthcare business and let it operate by supply and demand. The quality and availability of healthcare would improve, and costs would fall significantly.

Reduce income tax rates, especially for corporations. U.S. corporate tax rates are among the highest in the world. Excessive rates are a key reason why the economy is moribund and why so many jobs have left America. Relatively few years after a significant cut in tax rates, revenues would climb to new levels.

Reduce federal regulations. Since the start of the George W. Bush administration in 1991, federal regulators have imposed 1200 *major* rules – those that incur costs of at least $100 million each. Mr. Trump intends to reduce this burden.

Place limits on the Federal Reserve Bank. The Fed has gone hog wild imposing unnecessary requirements and regulations on financial institutions. Reforming monetary policy might render higher tariffs unnecessary.

Repeal the Dodd-Frank Act, which has provided no lasting benefits but caused considerable harm.

Amend civil service laws so that government workers can more easily be fired.

Stop paying the United Nations for measures to defeat global warming, and stop paying money in any regard to lessen atmospheric CO2. In the long run, fossil fuels may become less consequential as technology develops ways to generate electricity without producing CO2. Too much of the personal income of scientists comes from grants that are supplied by the government, causing science to become politicized.

Close the door on Muslims entering America. In Europe, Protestants and Catholics killed each other for several hundred years. Muslims should be given time to halt religious killings – in *their* lands, not ours. It would be nice to admit only peaceful Muslims, but one can't differentiate between those who intend to cause harm and those who don't.

A wall on the U.S. southern border is unlikely to be built, because neither Congress nor Mexico wants to pay for it. Besides, we already have a wall, not to mention 21,000 immigration agents. Far better to enforce the immigration laws already in place but not currently enforced. Here's a good start: People who enter the U.S. illegally and commit other crimes should be deported immediately.

It seems likely that Donald Trump will mature on the job, become increasingly presidential, with his policies becoming increasingly popular. America has 10 million more people working for government than in manufacturing. One hopes this ratio will be reversed.

DONALD TRUMP WILL BE A SUCCESS

February 4. 2017. Donald Trump will go down as a fine president.

America must, as he said, remove power from Washington and give it to the people. The most important measures: reduce tax rates and cut regulations.

Setting up an international gold standard is also important. This will solve many of the trade problems Mr. Trump objects to.

All tariffs are unwise. Studies have determined that a nation that has no tariffs will grow faster than opposing nations that have tariffs. The experience of Hong Kong, as explained in Chapter 11, bears this out.

The Civil Service Code should be amended, enabling federal bureaucrats to be fired.

It took several hundred years for Protestants and Catholics to stop killing each other. Let the Muslims fight it out in their own lands, not ours. They will probably calm down in a few decades. Until then, Muslims should not be admitted to America.

The U.S. military needs rebuilding. And our infrastructure needs work. Where will the money come from? From lower tax rates, reduction of regulations, and a gold standard. These will make the economy soar.

Best of all, the poor will benefit even more than the rich.

TRUMP'S CHINA TRADE POLICY IS CORRECT

September 10, 2018. President Trump is correct about U.S.-China trade. China's discrimination against us should be stopped. Over the years, America has helped China in many ways, as follows:

- In 1900, America's insistence on an "Open Door" policy prevented China from becoming colonized by European powers.

- Before and during World War II, the U.S. helped China defend against Japan.

- After the war, we ensured that China become one of the five permanent members of the UN Security Council.

- President Nixon's famous trip established bilateral ties with China.

- After Mao's death, the U.S. granted China favorable trade terms.

- President Carter gave China most-favored-nation trading status. President Reagan exempted China from trade restrictions applying to other communist countries.

- President George H.W. Bush made China's normal trade relations permanent and enabled it to join the World Trade Organization.

Yet China's tariffs have remained almost three times higher than U.S. tariffs. China should stop stealing American technology and stop engaging in electronic sabotage. President Trump has raised U.S. tariffs to pressure China into making its relationship with us more equitable. He has chosen economist David Malpass as his representative for China trade. I am familiar with Mr. Malpass and have great respect for him.

PRESIDENTIAL PRIORITIES

May 17, 2018. After reading my column lauding President Trump's policies, a friend wrote: "I disapprove of Trump. He's a terrible role model for young people. Would you want your daughter to become involved with this shell of a man?"

Of course not. But America's presidents, with the exception of a rapist, have been reasonably good people. Unfortunately, they feared the press, which is an offshoot of the Democratic Party, if not its leader. As a result, the government grew and grew, enabling politicians, bureaucrats, and their cronies to do well, but leaving the rest of us behind.

We now have in office a boor and a narcissist who is not just unafraid of the press, he delights in taunting the press. But he's making the economy come alive, leaving the rich unharmed but benefiting the rest of us, especially blacks, even more. He's also starting to knock back the bureaucracy. (Completing that little job will take decades.)

You can have your presidents of good character. I'll take good policies.

Another friend told me, "I disliked Trump's reversal of President Obama's environmental regulations."

Those regulations would have had no effect whatever on world temperature, but they certainly did slow down the economy. President Obama used environmental issues to disguise his main goals: to curtail capitalism and launch European-style socialism.

Liberty and limited government are the essential ingredients that have made America exceptional. Mr. Obama considered America unexceptional and, in fact, immoral. He wanted liberty reduced and government's powers much increased. Barack Obama is a very nice gentleman whose presidential goals and policies were un-American and unconstitutional in the extreme.

PRESIDENTIAL QUALIFICATIONS

July 29, 2019. After a recent column suggested winning policies for President Trump's second term, a Republican friend wrote, "Donald Trump stole creative property of my daughter's and refused compensation even after he was caught. He's a disaster and a disgrace!"

No one can blame my friend for his opinion.

Presidential qualifications, however, are different from personal morality. Both of the Bushes were nice people but middling presidents. Barack Obama is an exceptionally pleasant gentleman, but his socialism and opposition to capitalism made him a dreadful president.

I want a candidate who's unafraid of the media and has the desire and capability to cut tax rates, cut regulations, and reduce the government's size. I don't care if he's an uncouth, oversensitive narcissist. He'd get my vote even if he's a lying, cheating, thieving Darth Vader.

Mr. Trump has faltered on reducing government's size. One hopes for improvement on that score.

Soon after Gerald Ford became president in 1974, I commented on a radio show, "Government generally causes more harm than good. The press characterizes Mr. Ford as slow and incompetent. If this is true, the government would cause harm more slowly and less effectively, and that would be a net gain." The talk show host laughed heartily.

Before the Civil Service was created in 1883, America had the spoils system, whereby the president could hire government workers at will. This brought in possibly incompetent people for short-term employment. Civil Service brings in competent people for long-term employment. But the more competent the government workers and the longer they remain, the more damage they do. I prefer the spoils system, thank you.

RENEWING AMERICA

December 30, 2019. A friend wrote, "Trump's vulgar language, lack of morals, tweets, and his disregard of the laws of the land make him unfit to hold the office of president. He's an embarrassment, and should be removed by whatever means available."

Trump is an uncouth, oversensitive narcissist, but he has complied with the nation's laws.

His obsession with the nation's trade imbalance is foolish and unnecessary. Tariffs are unwise. For a large part of its history, America has run trade deficits without seriously inhibiting development. Other Trump policies, however, have brought us a roaring economy with black and Hispanic employment at all-time highs. Lower corporate tax rates, fewer antibusiness regulations, and the appointment of numerous relatively young constitutionalists to federal courts has been especially beneficial.

If the Senate tries President Trump, he will be exonerated. In November 2020, he will enjoy a landslide victory, and Republicans will probably control both houses of Congress. They can then begin truly draining the swamp.

Only two people I know of, Donald Trump and Rush Limbaugh, create joyful excitement when speaking about public affairs to large audiences. Both are unafraid of the press and can galvanize the nation into making big cuts in government spending.

Transcripts of Limbaugh's radio shows (rushlimbaugh.com) reveal that, once you're past the braggadocio, Rush is knowledgeable and has excellent judgment. He would win the 2024 presidential election handily. Taking office at just shy of 74 years old, Rush would make the U.S. government smaller and less intrusive. Trump and Limbaugh together could generate an American renewal, including higher morale, more peacefulness, and greater equality of wealth.

Shortly after the above column was published, Limbaugh announced he had been diagnosed with late-stage cancer. Without a complete, miraculous recovery, his running for president, sadly, seems out of the question.

TRUMP POLICIES NARROWED THE WEALTH GAP

September 27, 2020: Every three years, the Federal Reserve Bank publishes a Survey of Consumer Finance. The one published yesterday reveals a stark contrast between the Obama and Trump administrations.

From 2016 to 2019, families at the top income level experienced very little, if any, growth in net worth. But families at the bottom level experienced substantial gains. Mr. Trump's policies thus caused wealth to become more equal.

The opposite occurred from 2013 to 2016, during the Obama administration. The net worth of those in the top income level gained substantially more than that of the bottom level.

The long-term results of most government policies are counterintuitive. They're intended to help the poor, but they generally help the rich instead.

CONSTITUTIONAL COMPLIANCE

May 7, 2018. Some maintain that Mr. Trump has acted unconstitutionally. This hasn't been evident to me. If he had colluded with Russia about the 2016 election, the information would long since have been leaked.

President Obama's regulations by executive order without legislative approval was certainly unconstitutional. The regulations also dragged down the economy, which was especially damaging to the poor. The purpose of the Constitution is to limit government powers. Obama preferred unlimited powers. The Constitution was not his favorite document. Much more to his liking were the writings of socialist, political activist, and community organizer Saul Alinsky.

Hillary Clinton invited those who sought her favor when she later became president to fork over to the Clinton Charitable Foundation, from which she paid her campaign costs. These weren't bribes, I suppose, but they were close. Hillary also transferred to her personal computer and later destroyed thousands of documents, some of which contained government secrets. "Gosh, I didn't know that was illegal."

The regulations of the Consumer Financial Protection Bureau (CFPB) are not subject to review by the U.S. Legislature. The CFPB also obtains its money only from the Federal Reserve Bank. Bypassing the legislature so egregiously is unconstitutional. Congress is finally correcting this, arranging for legislative review of CFPB rulings and for legislative funding.

Mr. Trump has initiated a big reduction in the top corporate tax rate and reversed especially damaging regulations. He has placed constitutionalists on the Supreme Court and the courts of appeals. As a result, the economy has come alive, with blacks gaining faster than whites. So what if he's a narcissist? What counts are his policies.

ATTEMPTED COUPS AGAINST DONALD TRUMP[66]

December 16, 2019. The following were illegal efforts to undermine the election of Donald Trump and remove him from office:

- Hillary Clinton and the Democratic National Committee paid millions of dollars to former British spy Christopher Steele, who prepared a dossier smearing Trump using fake Russian sources.

- When James Comey and Attorney-General Loretta Lynch presented the Steele dossier to a FISA court to obtain warrants for spying on the Trump campaign, they failed to inform the court of the dossier's political origins.

---

66. Amgreatness.com, *When Does It Count as a Coup?* 10/20/19.

- CIA Director John Brennan and FBI Director James Comey initiated America's first-ever counterintelligence operation against a U.S. presidential candidate. Hundreds of agents endeavored to entrap members of the Trump campaign and link them to Russia.

- John Brennan circumvented the law by using British intelligence to target Trump.

- Contractors used the surveillance capabilities of the National Security Agency to spy on the Trump campaign.

- The Democratic National Committee sent a Ukrainian American, Alexandra Chalupa, to the Ukrainian embassy in Washington to coordinate smears against candidate Trump.

- Obama's Ukraine ambassador, Marie Yovanovitch, illegally instructed her team in Kyiv and the State Department in Washington to monitor leading American journalists and conservatives, including Sean Hannity, Lou Dobbs, and Donald Trump, Jr.

Peter Strzok, head of the FBI's counterintelligence division, participated in a conspiracy to undermine a Trump presidency.

These attempts to subvert the electoral will of the people deserve prosecution.

SECOND-TERM GOALS FOR PRESIDENT TRUMP[67]

July 15, 2019. Here are winning goals for Mr. Trump's second term:

- Revamp the scope, seniority, and unionization of the federal bureaucracy.

- Improve the permit process to speed up infrastructure work.

- Cut individual income tax rates. (The deficit was increased

---

67. WSJ, Kimberley A. Strassel, *Make America Even Greater*, 6/21/19.

because of additional spending, not because of the 2017 rate cut.)

- Index capital gains for inflation.

- Repeal the thousands of laws and regulations that can land citizens in jail without their even knowing they've committed a crime.

- Promote former House Speaker Paul Ryan's idea of making block grants to the states to cover food stamps and other anti-poverty measures, enabling the states to innovate and encourage people to work.

- Promote the elimination of state and local rules that block the construction of housing.

- Encourage the repeal of civil asset forfeitures by police departments.

- Encourage school choice and technical schools.

- Promise to continue naming constitutionalist Supreme Court nominees who would interpret laws but not make laws from the bench.

- Push for term limits on U.S. legislators.

- Close the wretched Federal Reserve Bank and remove the government's monopoly over the dollar.

Promulgating these goals would help Mr. Trump win a second-term victory.

BE BOLD, DONALD!

August 24, 2020. Andy Kessler has suggested[68] that President Trump highlight these policy changes:

68. WSJ, Andy Kessler, *A 'Yuge' Re-Election Agenda*, 7/19/20.

Abolish public-sector unions. The unions would squawk, but thousands of plain folks would flock to Trump's side.

Propose unlimited charter schools everywhere. The unions would complain, but thousands of blacks, seeking better education for their children, would love it.

Raise the Social Security retirement age. Most retirees recognize the necessity.

Buy Cuba. How so, you ask: The U.S. would pay $10,000 to each of Cuba's eleven million people. That would cost $110 billion – peanuts among today's monumental agendas. Give each Cuban a voucher for a share of Cuba's state-owned businesses. These would trade at increasing prices, as occurred in Eastern Europe, in anticipation of the companies being sold or going public. After the Commies flee, make Cuba a county of Florida.

(A friend to whom I showed this column, asked, "Why should the U.S. buy Cuba?" His skepticism rings true. America is probably large enough already.)

Terminate crony capitalist subsidies for oil, gas, solar, wind, ethanol, and electricity. Stop subsidizing staple commodities, like corn, which is weakening the American people by causing widespread obesity. Abolish Davis-Bacon to cut construction costs. Give the Jones Act the deep six to increase shipping in U.S. waters.

Change of Subject: What percentage of Americans have died from COVID-19?

Answer: just 1/20th of one percent, far fewer than the media wants us to believe. COVID-19 is not all that deadly. People under 70 in fairly good health and not obese are unlikely to die from it. Of those infected, more than 97% recover. Shutting down state economies was a grave mistake.

PREDICTION

This prediction, made by me on July 13, 2020, appears near the end of Chapter 4 and is repeated here:

"The polls in this month of July 2020 show President Trump losing soundly to Vice President Biden. I nevertheless predict that Donald Trump will be reelected in November 2020."

Chapter 10 – Miscellaneous

Government Programs Hurt the Poor

August 10, 2020: When told the title of this book, Linda said, "You should approach Bernie Sanders and Black Lives Matter. They want to help the poor too."

Black Lives Matter doesn't seem to be in the business of helping others. But yes, Bernie Sanders wants to aid the poor in the same way governments have tried to do for more than a century: Apply force with laws and regulations. Government is the only part of society that's authorized to use force. The actual, long-term results of government's use of force, in my observation, are opposite to the intended results.

The federal government has some 85 programs to help the poor. The gap between rich and poor has widened nevertheless.

This book highlights 38 ways that American governments make life harder and more expensive for the poor. Federal attempts to improve the economy are the most damaging, causing severe downturns that have devastated the poor.

The bureaucrats remain unaware that applying force usually fails. Force is their thing. They're loathe to give it up. Let's give *them* up and abolish the Civil Service System.

Government should become significantly smaller and less intrusive. If it stopped trying to help the poor and stopped aiding the rich with crony capitalism, the poor would gain wealth faster than the rich.

Nice change. Let's try it.

WHAT IF PORTLAND GAVE JOBS TO PANHANDLERS?

April 1, 2017. Liberals have good intentions. Most of them believe that governmental force is the correct way to deal with social and economic problems. "Force" being an unhappy word, liberals seldom use it. They refer instead to laws and regulations. But if you fail to obey a law or regulation, you're punished. It's force, all right. As George Washington rightly noted, "Government is force."

Recently, the government of Portland, Maine, decided that begging in the city streets, called panhandling, was a problem. Officials considered giving the panhandlers jobs, such as cleaning up city parks. Let's assume for a moment that such a law was enacted.

The city would exert two kinds of force: First, it requires residents to pay taxes to cover the panhandle payments. Second, the city requires that non-panhandlers not be hired for jobs that are intended for panhandlers. There's no choice about it. Only the people who enacted the law have the choice.

Okay, city taxes bring in money. The panhandlers get some of it, and liberals feel good about their intentions. What happens next?

People who haven't previously considered themselves panhandlers, but are unemployed, start carrying signs identifying themselves as genuine panhandlers. They let it be known they want city jobs too.

After the city accommodates them, panhandlers in other cities hear that Portland is where it's at. The city is inundated with them.

The panhandlers broaden their scope and start begging, even aggressively. Prosperous residents can hardly step outside without being accosted for money. Taxes are raised to pay all the panhandlers. No longer is Portland a pleasant place to live. The prosperous move elsewhere, the city deteriorates, and liberals wonder how government can straighten out the mess and still care for the poor panhandlers.

Portland would not allow such deterioration. The law was not enacted, and I dearly hope it won't be. (Comment in October 2020: This column comes uncomfortably close to the bone of the benighted City of San Francisco.)

But what if the major recipients of government largess are unionized government workers? What if their pensions have been raised to exorbitant levels because unions, supported by federal laws, are wealthy enough to pay substantial campaign gifts to legislators?

Gentle reader, I give you Detroit, Baltimore, and Chicago, all of which have had liberal leadership for decades and have lost significant populations.

I hazard the following generalizations:

- The actual, long-term results of big government policies are opposite to the intended results.

- Lobbying generally does not cause big government; it results from it.

- Instead of government welfare, private organizations should solicit money from the prosperous and pay most of it, usually with conditions, to the poor. The results would be better than government could accomplish, with far lower costs.

BUREAUCRATIC BUNGLING

October 23, 2017. Business managers usually take responsibility to get the job done right and satisfy customers. They also strive for profits, which depend partly on cutting costs.

To avoid blame, government officials avoid taking personal responsibility. Having no profits, they have every incentive to raise costs, because the bigger an official's budget, the higher his self-esteem. Seldom fired, bureaucrats give a low priority to pleasing the public.

Here's a real-life example of government bungling, high costs, and lack of caring:[69]

New York State was a young woman's original home. She had a New York license and retained it while attending school in Indiana. After graduation, she intended to move to California. But before her departure, she received a speeding ticket.

She mailed a check to pay the fine. But whoops, the Indiana court accepted payments only by credit card, not checks. Uncashed, her check was returned to her Indiana address. This she was unaware of, having already moved. Indiana notified New York of her failure to pay the speeding ticket.

Many years later, the woman moved back to New York and applied for a new license. New York wanted the Indiana fine paid first. She did so, and Indiana mailed New York a letter saying that her case had cleared.

Sorry, New York didn't accept letters, only faxes.

Sorry, Indiana didn't send faxes, only letters.

She asked the Indiana court to send an official document saying that the case had cleared. Sorry, the Indiana court couldn't do this and suggested that New York call the court.

Sorry, New York made no phone calls on driver license questions.

The woman obtained a receipt showing the Indiana ticket number and confirming that the fine had been paid. This she faxed to New York. Six weeks later, three months in all, still no response.

By its very nature, government, far more than business, is prone to bungling, high costs, and lack of caring.

---

69. I'm sorry I didn't save this WSJ article, written by the woman who had suffered the experience and was still suffering it at the time of the writing.

THE UNSEEN EFFECT OF PARENTAL LEAVE

August 7, 2017. Paid parental leave is the favorite issue of Number One Daughter, Ivanka Trump. The law would apply to both mothers and fathers, although mothers would probably predominate. The child could be natural-born or adopted. The parent would receive a salary for up to eight weeks and be guaranteed a return to her job.

The obvious advantage: The child can bond with at least one of the parents.

The disadvantage: If the government pays the salaries, a tax must be imposed. We have enough taxes, thank you. Mr. Trump was hired to cut the darn things, not raise them.

If employers pay the salaries, this would impose a heavy burden for marginally successful companies. Higher unemployment would result.

The absence of an employee for months is disruptive to the business. Temporary employees would probably be necessary, requiring training at the employer's cost.

During the eight-week absence, markets and technologies change. The returning employee must be brought up to speed, also at the employer's cost.

Here's the primary unseen consequence: To save costs, employers would hire fewer women. Is this what you want, Ivanka?

WHY AMERICANS AREN'T MOVING

August 21, 2017. Americans are moving less frequently than before.[70] The percentage of people who moved across a county line in 2015 was just 4.1%, down from 7.7% in the late-1970s. This is preventing rural residents from obtaining better jobs, and it's limiting the supply of labor where jobs are plentiful, thereby raising prices.

70. Wall Street Journal (WSJ), 8/3/17.

Here are key reasons for the decline of mobility, all because of big government:

- Large land areas in metropolitan areas are restricted from development, raising the cost of urban housing and hurting the poor most. People don't move to where they'd like to go because apartment rental costs are prohibitive.

- The portion of jobs requiring licenses has risen five-fold since 1950. More than a fourth of U.S. workers now require a state license to do their jobs. A license in one state may or may not be transferable to another. Licenses provide revenue to the states, but they suppress competition and raise consumer prices. This hurts the poor most.

- To some extent in the last several decades, Americans have lost trust in one another. This is because government has enacted a myriad of laws and regulations that create an atmosphere of controversy and conflict.

- Government's attempt to take responsibility for the lives of citizens has made them less likely to take responsibility for their own actions.

Government impediments prevent Americans from moving to where the jobs are.

AMERICA MAY FAIL

December 3, 2018. America may fail permanently. Here's why:

- Most government policies have obvious, positive results in the short run. But voters are unaware that many policies have hidden negative results that greatly outweigh the positives. The actual, long-term results of big government policies, in my observation, are opposite to the intended results.

- The buildup of the national debt is becoming unmanageable.

- Society works best when citizens take responsibility for their actions. But scientists are identifying more and more causes of human feelings and actions, limiting the apparent scope of free will. This gives liberals more opportunities to remove responsibility from individuals and make government responsible.

- The more work performed by robots, the more human character deteriorates.

- The federal government and the Federal Reserve Bank have caused major economic downturns. For example, as described in Chapter 2, the 2008 recession was caused by unwise government policies. Government should do nothing about the economy. Liberals consider this unthinkable.

- Too many illegal immigrants from big government nations are voting for big government here in America.

- Liberals abhor the U.S. Constitution because it restrains their power. They want a "living" constitution, interpreted according to how the political winds are blowing.

- Liberals act as if everyone's a victim except healthy, prosperous, white, Anglo-Saxon, Protestant males. They promote identity politics, encouraging "victimized" groups to lobby for government help.

- Schools receive too much financial support from government. Too many young minds educated in those schools are full of mush. The following statement of Thomas Sowell certainly applies to schools: "Ideas that don't work are concentrated in institutions where ideas don't have to work to survive."

Two Serious Economic Misunderstandings

December 17, 2018. Most denizens of the government and the press believe that deflation (falling prices) results from a weak economy. To counteract this, the authorities try to keep interest rates low. But unnaturally low interest rates make borrowing too easy and often results in excessive debt.

Deflation during the Great Depression was indeed caused by a weak economy. But the other kind of deflation results from a strong economy, when the supply of goods grows more rapidly than the supply of money. Prices fall, and the economy thrives, helping the poor most. The Federal Reserve Bank thinks the current deflation stems from economic weakness. That's wrong: It stems from strength.

Another misunderstanding: The reduction of tax rates, referred to as "tax cuts," is believed to cause government revenues to fall, increasing the deficit. But the tax cut label, *implying* a reduction of government revenues, is misleading. Governments have no control over their tax revenues; it's the tax *rates* they control. When the rates are reduced, government takes a smaller share of peoples' incomes, which stimulates the economy. More people find work, income rises, and government revenues go up, not down. If government spending remains level, the higher revenues reduce the deficit.

When corporate tax rates were reduced at the beginning of 2018, Congress increased spending substantially. It was that additional spending, not the lower tax rates, that increased the deficit. The same thing happened in the 1980s, when President Reagan reduced income tax rates substantially. As a result, tax revenues doubled. But government spending *more* than doubled, causing the deficit to increase. Liberals blamed the deficit increase on the "tax cuts," but this was highly misleading.

Liberals thrive on lies. Except in the central cities, Americans are basically conservative. Only about 25% of Americans consider themselves liberals. Lying and cheating at the polls enable Democrats to gain traction. (At this writing in October 2020, I expect substantial increases in voting for Republicans among American blacks.)

Cutting tax rates is good policy. This year's reduction and the cancellation of damaging regulations are why the unemployment rate is the lowest it's been in fifty years. The government should cut tax rates more, especially individual income tax rates. It should also cancel more regulations. And, oh yes, spend less.

CALIFORNIA'S BIG GOVERNMENT[71]

June 1, 2020. California provides a good test of whether big government is the correct approach to solving social and economic problems.

California has the most billionaires of any state. That's a start.

It has the highest state income tax rates, the highest gasoline tax rates, and the highest sales tax rates. Should be plenty of money to solve problems, right?

Actually not. Whatever's taxed, you get less of. High tax rates on income, for example, results in less income.

Let's see other results:

- California's public schools rate in the lowest 10% of the nation's test scores.

- With welfare payments high, one-third of the nation's welfare recipients live in California.

- 140,000 people in California live on the street.

- California provides considerable help to the poor and homeless. Whatever you subsidize, you get more of. Surprise, surprise; one-fifth of the nation's homeless live in California.

---

71. This column is based on verbal statements by Victor David Hanson on the 6/18/19 Tucker Carlson Show. The title of the interview was *California is America's First Third-World State*. I obtained a transcript of the comments and then heard the show directly.

- One-fifth of the population is below the poverty line. Generally, California has the largest underclass of any state.

Maybe California favors the French approach. When a theory and facts are in conflict, the French tend to favor the theory. California's theory says that big government is the best approach to equitable prosperity. The facts say otherwise. California continues to go for the theory.

Every year for the last 20 years, more people have left the state than moved into it.

GOVERNMENT RAISES COSTS

(This column was written in 2019.) There is much talk these days about increasing the role of government. Some believe that getting rid of private sector profits would cut costs.

The truth is quite the opposite: Government raises costs; the private sector reduces them. In the private sector, profits, competition, and the possibility of being fired keeps costs down. A business owner who fails to keep track of his costs is likely to be underpriced by competitors and may fail altogether. A manager who allows costs to rise is subject to being fired.

Government has neither profits nor competition, and its bureaucrats are rarely fired. Government provides little check on its costs.

After a problem has been solved, people in the private sector stop funding it because the solution is no longer profitable. But bureaucrats prefer not to solve problems, because this would make their jobs unnecessary. For example, the federal government offers something like 80 programs to help the poor. The gap between rich and poor, however, has not diminished. If anything, it has grown.

Federal legislators use other people's money to bestow benefits, most of which have a big impact on the people being helped. But the cost of each benefit adds only pennies to the tax paid by the average citizen. The benefits to the few are obvious. The per capita costs to the many are small and hidden.

When government offers a benefit, people arrange their affairs to obtain it. Businesses, for example, replace engineers with lawyers. Such reactions perpetuate the elevation of costs.

The prosperous tend to gain wealth faster than the poor because the prosperous induce government to help them. This crony capitalism sustains government spending and widens the gap between rich and poor.

No segment of the U.S. economy is more costly than the federal government. It has accumulated an unbelievable $25 trillion dollars of debt. This will eventually trigger a severe economic downturn, which will be especially hard on the poor.

A bigger role for the government would raise costs substantially.

THE RESULTS OF GOVERNMENT FORCE ARE COUNTERINTUITIVE

Government is the only element of society that's permitted to use force. Laws and regulations are backed by force. The purposes may be desirable, but many of the long-term results, usually unseen, are counterintuitive and damaging. Here are examples:

- Forcing the income of low-wage workers higher with minimum wage causes people who have little experience and few skills to have difficulty finding jobs. The income of current employees can be counted, but not the lost income of people who were not hired.

- Government welfare, which can be counted, creates dependency, which cannot.

- The federal government and the Federal Reserve purport to

make the economy less volatile, but they fail. They contributed greatly to the Great Depression, the 1974 recession, and the 2009 Great Recession. If they would just let the economy alone, downturns would become far less severe, helping the poor most.

- Union wages raise the income for members, but increase prices for everyone. The poor are hurt the most, because they're generally not union members, but they spend the biggest portion of their income on living expenses.

- When the government provides flood insurance whose premiums are unrealistically low, more and more people want to own homes in areas that are prone to flooding.

- California's laws and regulations have provided significant help for the homeless. Could be a reason why so many of the nation's homeless now live in California.

Unaware of the counter-intuitive effects of their policies, leaders cause harm without realizing it.

Most U.S. education is funded by government. Accordingly, voters generally remain in the dark about the harm caused by government.

CHARLOTTESVILLE

The rioting in Charlottesville, Virginia in August 2017 provided liberals with the opportunity to imply that America is riddled with white supremacists and Nazis.

It is not. Columns by Holman Jenkins,[72] a prominent Wall Street Journal columnist, imply that the rioting was exacerbated by the Charlottesville city government. This judgment is based on a report by Hunton & Williams, LLP, commissioned by the city, and issued five months after the 2017 rioting occurred. The Hunton & Williams report

72. WSJ, Holman W. Jenkins, Jr., *Every Protester Has a Reason*, 6/3/20, and WSJ, Holman W. Jenkins, Jr., *How Free Speech Lost in Charlottesville*, 12/5/17.

revealed that the City of Charlottesville issued a permit to a group of white supremacists and then allowed the local police chief to deliberately withhold protection, enabling a riot to develop that the state police would then be justified in breaking up.

Way to keep the peace, city officials. You really know how to limit violence to the lowest possible level.

FAULTY POLICE INVESTIGATIONS[73]

June 2, 2020. Following the murders of blacks by white police officers, faulty investigations have followed, resulting in spikes in violent crimes.

It happened in Ferguson, MO, after an officer shot Michael Brown. It happened in Chicago after a cop killed Laquan McDonald. And it happened in Baltimore after Freddie Gray was killed in custody.

Public demonstrations went viral after these events. As a result, the federal government under the Obama administration became involved. Instead of individual policemen being investigated and charged, entire police departments were put under a cloud. Instead of investigations of police departments being done locally *with* the police, they were done by the feds *to* the police.

Investigators have also failed to provide balanced views about police killings of blacks. The Washington Post database reveals that a police officer is 18½ times more likely to be killed by a black male than an unarmed black male is to be killed by a police officer.

Following each of these faulty investigations, the policemen in those cities understandably have curbed their interactions with civilians. The result: Homicides and total crimes have risen considerably after each of these faulty investigations, leading to numerous additional deaths and

---

73. WSJ, Jason L. Riley, *Good Policing Saves Black Lives,* 6/2/20, and WSJ, Heather Mac Donald, *The Myth of Systemic Police Racism,* 6/3/20.

other difficulties, mostly in black communities. Thanks for all the help, feds.

The Best Way to Help the Poor

Most conservatives maintain that a growing economy is a good way to help the poor. They're right; it's a good way. But it's not the best way.

The poor are down because government, without meaning to, keeps them down. (See Chapters 1, 2, and 3.) Get government to back off, and the poor will pull themselves up remarkably quickly.

Curing Innovation Famine[74]

Plenty of innovation is going on in the digital world. But the non-digital world of Western nations suffers from innovation famine. Quick-witted Peter Thiel observed, "Bits are lightly regulated. Atoms are heavily regulated."

Non-digital innovation is suppressed for two reasons: government licensing and the patent process.

1. Government licensing is too burdensome and slow. A 2012 study, for example, found that a medical device takes around 21 months to get through the regulatory process in the U.S., not to mention 90 months in Germany.

Government regulation is not only expensive, it's unnecessary. If a product doesn't work, the people who first use it will discover the problem, causing the developer to return to the drawing board. Tinkering is usually the best path to progress.

If a product is unsafe and someone gets hurt, the developer may be sued. Lawsuits are expensive and problematic. Developers are likely to make sure that products are safe from the beginning.

---

74. WSJ, Matt Ridley, *Restoring the Freedom to Experiment,* 5/16/20.

The regulating bureaucrat says, "We want to make sure that no one wastes money on faulty products and that even from the get-go, no one gets hurt."

Oh, you want to ensure perfection, do you? Have you counted the number of people who became ill or died during the 21 months they weren't able to use that medical product? You didn't, eh? Have you considered that the developer is probably a better tinkerer than you are? Surprise, surprise; during those 21 months, she may have developed improvements you couldn't dream of. Innovators are in the business of innovating. You're in the business of applying force and fabricating lies to make you feel good about it.

2. Innovation famine in the non-digital world is also caused by the patent process, which is slow, expensive, and unnecessary. A 2002 study by Josh Lerner, an economist at Harvard Business School, looked at 177 cases in 60 countries over more than a century during which the patent policies were strengthened. He found that the policy changes did not spur innovation.

James Watt, Samuel Morse, Guglielmo Marconi, the Wright brothers, and many others wasted many years in court defending their intellectual property when they might have been perfecting their products instead.

3-D printing is one example among many: The lapse of patents resulted in substantial improvements in quality and declines in price.

In developing nickel-iron batteries, Thomas Edison's employees conducted 50,000 experiments. As Edison famously said, developing new technology is "1 percent inspiration and 99 percent perspiration."

In all these examples, the initial discoveries would probably have been realized even if the patent system had not existed. Patenting is just government exerting power for no good purpose. Trial and error is the best path to innovation. It's more fruitful and probably more profitable than trying to protect what a person has already created.

The famine of innovation would be lifted if government regulation and government patenting in the Western world were abolished.

IMPOSSIBLE TECHNOLOGIES

October 3, 2020. Fifty years ago, some of today's technologies were considered impossible. Here are future possibilities most people consider impossible now:

- Circumventing death and disease. Nanotechnologists today are making things that do the work ever smaller. Perhaps 30 years from now, might it not be possible for us to consume millions of microscopic computers, each of which can grasp, move, and communicate? A cloud of them would live permanently in our bodies, fixing whatever needs fixing. We could direct them to make our biological age younger permanently, but without diminishing the knowledge and judgment we had accumulated at the older age. I've never read science fiction, but I don't consider this impossible.

- Einstein proved some of Newton's views wrong. Why couldn't some of Einstein's views eventually be proven wrong? With quantum physics and the help of extraordinary robots, mankind might learn to travel faster than the speed of light. People and things would be able to travel billions of light years in a flash without deterioration.

Developing this tricky maneuver would probably take longer than 30 years. But with people continuing to have children and not dying, things could get testy without some means of escape.

If we can't find another planet similar to earth, we might create one. It would be fun to see how the robots accumulate many cubic miles of white-hot iron at the core. Building another earth would cost a little extra, but anything's possible.

ELECTIONS ARE CHEAP

December 2, 2016. People are unnecessarily concerned about the cost of elections. The Center for Responsive Politics, which tracks money and lobbying in elections, says the 2016 election cost $6.9 billion. Call it $7 billion.

The national income is $17 trillion.

$7 billion is only 4 hundredths of one percent (.04%) of the $17 trillion national income. That means 1/25th of one percent of the national income is utilized to choose the nation's leaders without bloodshed. We're talking peanuts! And this cost is incurred only every four years, during presidential elections. The costs are less during intervening years. How fortunate we are that elections cost so little! They're a whole lot cheaper than civil war. (Comment added in 2020: Civil war is what Black Lives Matter seems inclined to encourage.)

This book recommends that members of the U.S. House and Senate be limited in office to one term each, with their pay sharply reduced. If America was so blessed as to enact such measures, the cost of elections would decline significantly because people would seek those offices as a temporary duty, an act of giving, not to be political professionals and get rich. (Have you noticed how often members of the House and Senate become millionaires? I wonder how this happens, since they hotly maintain, when they seek higher pay, that the cost of office is a tremendous financial burden.)

Okay, back to my story: The presidential election in 2016 cost $7 billion. How long does it take for the federal government to spend $7 billion?

Let's see. The estimated federal spending for the fiscal year 2016 was $3.854 trillion.

A 365-day year contains 8,760 hours.

$3,854 trillion divided by 8,760 hours means that the government spends almost $440 million an hour.

At $440 million an hour, the government spends $7 billion in about 16 hours.

Now *that's* something worth worrying about.

GET MONEY OUT OF POLITICS?

Get money out of politics, right? That's what liberals maintain, anyway. Their actual goal is to get *Republicans* out of politics, so the liberals can have the power and control the money that goes with the power.

But liberals have succeeded in sharply limiting the amount of money each of us deplorables can give as campaign gifts. This makes it hard for plain folks to run for office. It opens the door for wealthy people, plain or not, to run and win.

Yes, get money out of politics, except if you're already loaded. Then it's okay.

AMERICA'S MIDDLE CLASS HAS MOVED UP[75]

October 7, 2019. America's middle class is shrinking. But it has moved up, not down.

A study publicized by the American Institute of Economic Research defines the middle class as those Americans whose annual income, measured in constant 2017 dollars, is between $35,000 and $100,000. During the 51 years from 1967 to 1997, the percentage of middle-income households fell from 53.8% to 41.3%.

But they didn't become poorer. No, during that same half-century, the portion of households with income *under* $35,000 also shrank, falling from 37.2% to 29.5%.

Instead, the middle class became richer. Households with income over $100,000 more than tripled, from 9.0% to 29.2%.

---

75. AIER, Donald J. Boudreaux, *Have Two-Income Households Made Us Poorer?* 8/12/19.

More women are working, yes. But the percentage of working women peaked in 1995. During the two decades that followed, middle-class income continued higher even though the percentage of working women remained about level.

Since 1967, technology has alleviated the work performed by stay-at-home women. Microwaves, automatic dishwashers, and other increasingly reliable appliances have enabled women to devote less time to household work and obtain outside jobs instead.

In the mid-1960s, Americans spent about 15% of their disposable income on food. Now, despite a far higher percentage of meals consumed in restaurants, the portion is less than 10%.

These trends are triumphs of free market capitalism.[76]

Government has become deeply involved in education, healthcare, and housing. The prices in those sectors have risen especially fast. But this was just coincidental, of course.

SOCIAL SECURITY IS A FRAUD

March 9, 2020. Social Security is the biggest and grandest Ponzi scheme the world has ever known.

The money paid in Social Security taxes is immediately paid out to retirees, with any excess going to whatever the federal government is funding that day. The money is not invested in a trust fund, as it would be with an insurance policy.

Oh, there's a trust fund all right, but it contains no money and never has. The fund does contain over a trillion dollars of Treasury IOUs. Will those eventually be paid?

Of course not. When Social Security got started in the 1930s, there

---

76. This column is not about America's poor. America's monstrous government keeps the poor down. Most of their income is not earned. More generally, the quality of American life is deteriorating, and the national debt has become mountainous. Let's try the libertarian approach for a century or so and see how it feels. If I remain content with life, I might still be alive then.

were forty workers for every retiree. Now, there are only 2.9 workers, and the number of retirees continues to grow faster than that of the workers. In about ten years, there will be only two workers for every retiree.

When politicians try to raise Social Security taxes, the workers will respond, "You want me to pay half the cost of a retiree? The hell I will!" And they will throw the taxing politicians out of office.

Social Security is a transfer of funds from young to old. When the retirement costs of the elderly become too burdensome for the young, the system fails.

Raising the age at which Social Security benefits begin would help, but not for long. The entire system is fraudulent. For those not retired, it should be privatized and converted into true insurance, with the money not needed immediately invested for the future. Ultimately, government should have nothing to do with pensions.

STOP THE CHAIN IMMIGRATION OF RELATIVES

January 15, 2018. About one million immigrants enter the United States each year. But only one in 15 comes because of a job offer or their skills. Many of them come because they're related to someone already here. Other relatives can then follow for the same reason.

In the last 50 years, 36 million immigrants have arrived because they're members of a family. Adding more than 24 million illegal immigrants makes some 60 million people, most of whom came to the USA because of something other than a specific job.

Congress is now considering the Raise Act, which reorients immigration away from the unlimited chain migration of relatives and toward skilled individuals who can contribute the most to America. The bill would especially help the disadvantaged. President Trump has encouraged its passage.

After the Civil War, the door was open wide for immigrants, causing wages to fall too low. The Pullman Strike of 1894, when 250,000 workers halted most railroad traffic, was key to the early development of unions. If the government had kept better control of immigration, the strike might not have occurred, and government-supported unions might not be the rich, powerful, independent fiefdoms they are today.[77]

When the federal government permits too many immigrants, wages fall, and unions arise to force them up again. When immigration is balanced, unions become less necessary.

HUMAN BEINGS: AN ENDANGERED SPECIES

June 27, 2018. Warren Buffett says that overpopulation is a problem.

He's right, but only if people can avoid dying. Without that tricky little undertaking, human beings face extinction.

To sustain the population, the number of children born to the average woman during her lifetime, called the fertility rate, must be 2.1.

In agricultural societies, children are assets. They help grow the crops and provide for the old age of parents.

But as people flock into cities and gain prosperity, children become liabilities. They get in the way and cost a ton of money. Armed with pensions and birth control pills, women in prosperous urban areas produce fewer babies.

Oh yes, the world's population, now 7.6 billion, is still growing and may reach 9 or 10 billion. But it will then decline. According to the CIA, the fertility rates of developed nations are below the 2.1 sustaining rate: The U.S. and UK 1.88. European Union 1.61, China, 1.60. Japan 1.41.[78]

The government of Singapore provides cash and benefits worth up to $12,000 for each of a woman's first and second child and up to

---

77. I obtained this information from the Web.
78. Information obtained from the Web.

$20,000 for each of the third and fourth child. Singapore's fertility rate nevertheless stands at a rock-bottom 0.83.[79] The women of Singapore are just having too much fun to bother with babies.

With rates of about 4.5, the fertility of many African nations is still high. But as Africans become prosperous, the fertility rate will fall.

Unless human beings can circumvent dying, they will eventually go the way of the dodo bird, probably to be replaced by robots.

TIDBITS

July 16, 2018. Mr. Zuckerberg has agreed to federal regulation of Facebook. And why not? The company can handle the extra costs, while some of its smaller competitors cannot. Facebook will be assured of continued domination. Consumers will be hurt by less innovation, less competition, higher prices, and bigger government. The winners will be Facebook and the regulators.

About half of the scientific studies relied on by the feds cannot be replicated.[80] For years, government has issued laws and regulations based on faulty scientific procedures, especially regarding global warming. Unfortunately, scientists have little incentive to replicate studies initially undertaken by others. There's little glory in it. If the initial study attracted attention, the replicator feels like an also-ran. Even if the initial study cannot be reproduced, the failure usually attracts little attention.

In 1890, federal, state and local governments spent 6.2% of the GDP. Now, the various U.S. governments are spending 35.5% of the GDP. But there's room for further growth, is there not? After all, the Soviet government spent 70% of the nation's GDP, and everyone knows what a success the Soviet Union was.

Before committing mass murder at a school in Parkland, Florida,

---

79. Ditto.
80. WSJ, Peter Wood & David Randall, *How Bad is the Government's Science?* 4/17/18.

Nicholas Cruz had a record of felonies as a public school student in St. Paul, Minnesota. But he was never arrested because the school sought to avoid the school-to-prison pipeline for troubled kids. It's a good thing Cruz wasn't sent to prison. That could have led to a life of crime.[81]

Of the 175 people arrested in Kenosha, Wisconsin for looting, smashing cars, and torching buildings, 105 were from outside the city. George Soros, wealthy Democrat, has paid for a number of these rent-a-mobs.

Football fans want to watch football, not listen to racism lectures.

Ludwig von Mises, prominent Austrian economist: The standard of living for the common man is highest in those countries that have the greatest number of wealthy entrepreneurs.

If liberals continue to increase the size and intrusiveness of government, the U.S. government will eventually have to stop paying its bills. Alternatively, it could create runaway inflation, making the debts become insignificant for the government. But the value of bonds, bank deposits, and insurance policies would become insignificant as well, devastating the finances of everyone else.

When the government has to borrow money just to pay the interest on the debt, we'll be close to America's financial cataclysm. We're not there yet, but the conditions are approaching.

Human society works best when citizens, presumed to have free will, are held responsible for their behavior. As scientists find more causes and effects in human behavior, government considers it necessary to take on ever more responsibilities. But a bigger and more intrusive government widens the gap between rich and poor and causes human society to deteriorate. We're better off *assuming* that our wills are free, even if they're not.

Liberals oppose charter schools and endorse defunding the police. They embrace vacuous statements like "systematic racism" and "white

---

81. Ann Coulter, *Secret Debate Tip for GOP,* 3/14/18.

supremacy," which provoke white guilt. These utterances strike no chord with members of the black underclass. They want their schools to be better and their streets to be safe, thank you.

PAY GAPS RESULT FROM EMPLOYEE CHOICES, NOT SEXISM[82]

April 22, 2019. A recent study examined data of the train and bus operators of the Massachusetts Bay Transportation Authority (MBTA). The male employees took home more money than the women, but the difference was due to employee choices, not sexism.

The MBTA is a union shop with uniform hourly wages for men and women. All employees adhere to the same rules and enjoy the same benefits. Promotions are based solely on seniority, not performance. Men and women with the same seniority have the same options for scheduling, routes, vacation, and overtime. The rigid work rules prevent managers from giving preferential treatment to men.

Here are conclusions of the study:

- At time-and-a-half pay, overtime had a significant effect on the earnings. The men worked 83% more overtime hours than the women and were twice as likely to accept an overtime shift on short notice. About twice as many women as men never worked overtime.

- Under the Family Medical Leave Act, men took 48% fewer unpaid hours off than women.

- Women disproportionately chose to take undesirable routes if it meant working fewer nights, weekends, and holidays.

- In comparison with childless workers, fathers worked more overtime and mothers took more time off.

82. WSJ Editorial, *Parsing the Gender Pay Gap*, 11/22/18.
WSJ Editorial, *'Equal Death Day': May 3, 2030,* 4/9/18.

Throughout the nation, women generally avoid high-paying jobs that are dangerous or require strength. They generally favor lower-paying fields. Mothers are more likely than fathers to choose flexibility over career advancement.

Nationwide, women are said to make 80 cents for every dollar made by men. This is probably true but in almost every case, it's due to personal choices, not sexism.

Liberals make a big deal of the 80-20 discrepancy, but pay no attention to the reasons. Facts matter not to them. They just want to push people around with more laws and regulations. They want the power, always more power.

DEREGULATION INCREASED PUBLIC OWNERSHIP OF STOCKS[83]

May 6, 2019. Under prior administrations, Securities and Exchange regulations of publicly held stocks were so onerous that many fledgling companies avoided public markets and obtained needed capital from the wealthy.

A new company needs an idea to work on, people to do the work, stuff to work with, and space to do it in. Considerable time passes before sales are sufficient to pay the company's costs. When the risks of new ventures are highest, the money often comes from savings, family, friends, and perhaps a few rich folks. But when a promising company needs substantial additional funds to build the business, it can obtain money by selling its stock (shares of ownership) to public investors.

Hold it, said the SEC of prior administrations. You have to comply with this requirement and that requirement. You have to incur heavy legal costs disclosing a preposterous amount of information few people read.

83. WSJ Editorial, *Startups Grow Up* 2/23/19 and WSJ, Jean Eaglesham and Coulter Jones, *Powering U.S. Business: Private Capital,* 4/3/18.

More and more companies, therefore, skipped public markets and obtained money from the wealthy through private funds not subject to regulations. The number of companies owned by public investors and traded in stock markets fell significantly, widening the gap between rich and poor.

The Jobs Act of 2012 began the process of deregulation. Yes, that was during the Obama administration, which generally favored more regulation, not less. Maybe he was having a bad day.

The Trump administration, with Congressional support, cut through considerably more regulations, enabling numerous additional companies to go public. The stocks of more companies, some large but mostly small, can now be publicly owned. It's a win for small investors and for the nation.

SAVING BASEBALL

July 1, 2019. For increasing numbers of Americans, baseball is boring. Endlessly watching the catcher and pitcher play catch doesn't do it. Baseball's lore and statistics will come to naught if people are unwilling to attend the games or watch them on television. The games need to be shorter, with more hits and more base-running. Otherwise, baseball will eventually disappear. Consider these changes:

- Get rid of the pitcher's mound. The pitcher should stand at the same level as the other players.

- Batters are out after four strikes, not three.

- Batters take first base after three balls, not four.

- Teams are allowed four outs in an inning.

- Teams are allowed only three pitching changes in the game.

- Without a tie, the game is complete after five innings.

- With a tie, the game continues for two more innings. An unbroken tie is recorded as a tie.

These changes will provide more base-running and higher scoring. Most people don't consider traditions or statistics in deciding whether to attend the games or watch them on TV. They want to be entertained. If the games aren't made shorter and more exciting, baseball will die.

I'm not holding my breath waiting for any such changes. Professional baseball loves its traditions and will hold them high even on the day the game goes into the dugout for the last time.

More Tidbits

Worldwide, some $13 trillion of bonds are currently priced to deliver yields of less than zero. Lenders don't receive interest; they pay it. Nothing like this has occurred in 4,000 years of recorded interest rate history.

Key foreign policy issues are conducted out of the White House. The State Department and its scores of costly embassies have become superfluous and should be closed. The U.S. consulates help tourists with visas and other matters. These are important functions, but surely there must be a way to separate consulates from the government.

Including benefits, Federal civil servants earn half as much again as workers with equivalent jobs in the private sector. The four richest counties in the United States are clustered around Washington, DC. The servants have become the masters.

It's devastating when prices fall because of widespread bankruptcies, as occurred during the Great Depression. But it's quite a different story, and highly favorable, when prices fall because rapid economic activity induces a flood of goods and services. This is probably occurring in the U.S. now.

It was okay for local governments to give cable companies monopolies, enabling them to recover the cost of laying cable. But the governments should have granted the monopolies for only ten years, not forever. The cable companies, free of competition indefinitely, can now charge outrageous prices without end.

9/11 Deaths Partly Caused by Regulators?

October 21, 2019. More than 3,000 people died when the Twin Towers fell in lower Manhattan on 9/11. Terrorists, of course, were responsible. But surprisingly enough, U.S. regulators may also have contributed to the disaster.

With pressure from the regulators, the Twin Towers were the first skyscrapers whose steel scaffolding was insulated with a material other than asbestos. When burning airplane fuel flooded the upper floors, the substitute insulation failed to prevent the steel from melting. The huge weight of the upper floors fell on the floors below. Even though the steel scaffolding of those floors had not melted, they failed anyway, one by one, because of the crushing weight from above.

Asbestos, treated by regulators as a no-no, would probably have prevented the scaffolding on the upper floors from melting long enough to allow people on lower floors to escape. Many lives would probably have been saved.[84]

Do you suppose government officials would take this as an indication that they should stop regulating buildings?

Are you daft? They wouldn't consider such a dreadful idea under any circumstances.

---

84. I obtained this information from the Web, where there was controversy as to whether asbestos would have saved the day or not. In my mind, the matter is too close for comfort. To be on the safe side, the use of asbestos to insulate scaffolding should be reinstated.

THE MEDIA'S CONFLICT OF INTEREST

May 4, 2020. Why does the media overwhelmingly favor big government?

Because free markets are boring. With hundreds of millions of people fulfilling their own needs, what's to report? When sex, misfortune, pathos, or wrongdoing is involved, fine, the media can jump on those. But humdrum living by just plain folks? Consumers don't watch television news for that.

Government is different. It's the only part of society authorized to use force. It impacts everyone, and it's loaded with secrets. Like kids wanting to know what mummy and daddy are doing behind their bedroom door, people pay to learn about government.

Big government, therefore, financially benefits the media. But except for those who work for government and its cronies, big government is bad for everyone else, especially the poor. The media is unaware of its conflict of interest.

SERBS AND CIGARETTES

Here's an example of a government policy resulting unintentionally in great human suffering.

Many Western nations taxed, and still tax, cigarettes, raising the prices thereof. Taxes tend to be especially high in Western Europe.

In 1992, the Serbian government acquired tons of cigarettes, some of poor quality, from local and international sources. With a fleet of planes, they smuggled the cigarettes into Western Europe, where the cigarettes, less expensive than the taxed variety, sold easily.

The Serbs used the profits to pummel the Bosnians. Western nations, including the U.S., reacted by bombing the Serbs.

If the Western Europeans had reduced their government spending and imposed no tax on cigarettes, the Serbs would not have had the money to attack the Bosnians, etc. etc.

The countries that taxed the cigarettes didn't intend all those consequences, of course. But government policies have far-reaching effects that are deleterious far more often than not.

TECHNOLOGY WILL REPLACE JOBS

A professional anthropologist (I didn't record her name) told me years ago: The technological advance of early man began slowly about two million years ago, when some smart cookies realized that if you take a stone that has an edge, the stone becomes more useful when you chip away the edge and make it sharper. This lasted about a million years. People then realized that if you chip the edge of a stone on both sides, it becomes even more useful. This lasted another million years.

After that plodding start, the development of technology has increased in speed ever since. Even the pace of change has itself speeded up.

A tidal wave of technology now approaches, having the capability to put all natural human beings out of work.

Robots will be able to do everything natural human beings can do. They will speak idiomatically and have all five senses, self-awareness, judgment, humor, and common sense. They will read, understand, and remember everything that's on the Web and every book that's ever been written, regardless of language. There won't be a single thing natural human beings can do that robots can't do better and cheaper, including manage companies, plan marketing campaigns, make speeches, write books, design buildings, paint pictures, compose music, and play concert piano.

Robots will create and teach other robots at the rate of billions of data a second. If you think human beings can keep up by taking courses, you're dreaming.

After robots persuade us that they can feel hurt, voting by robots will probably be authorized. This would herald the end for real human beings.

If the robots don't kill each other and technology continues to advance at an ever-faster pace, I believe our technological successors will gain control of the entire universe within a couple of centuries. They'll probably learn how to go faster than the speed of light or how to transport people and things billions of miles in an instant. (No, I do not read science fiction and never have.)

Most futurists have maintained that the advance of technology creates more employment than it replaces. But they haven't taken into account that, before long, robots will possess more capabilities in every way than natural human beings. For the first time, those who proclaim that the Luddites are wrong will themselves be wrong.

STILL MORE TIDBITS

Private parties influence the economy when they buy or sell financial securities. Competitors make opposite moves, usually negating the distortions. Having no competition, government's actions in financial markets create distortions that are not counteracted.

The National Rifle Association, founded in 1871, provided guns to blacks to protect themselves from the Ku Klux Klan. The NRA is America's oldest, continuously operating civil rights organization.

When politicians howl about racism, tell them, "You are the ones who are racists. You assume that blacks can't make it without government's help."

We should be allowed to take our own lives and to pay those who assist. But because of their conflicts of interest, people who work in healthcare should not be allowed to assist, because they are sworn to extend life, not shorten it. People in government should also be prevented from assisting suicides, because they might be especially enthusiastic about helping people who want to reduce the size of government kill themselves.

"Freedom" and "liberty" do not mean people can do whatever they want. The words mean freedom from unlimited government.

The Export-Import Bank should be closed. Using money taxed from American citizens, it pays welfare to big corporations, especially Boeing.

In 1967, when the war on poverty first got going, almost 70% of prime working-age adults in the bottom-fifth of households were employed. Now the working portion has fallen to only 36%. Are government welfare payments too high? Naah, couldn't be.

Instead of the federal government allocating stimulus payments to some parties and not to others, just suspend the payroll tax for everyone. That'll save money and get the government out of the allocation business.

Nuclear power plants, a wonderful way to reduce atmospheric CO2, are way too expensive.[85] They're not just required to protect against accidents, they're required to protect against trivial emissions. Coal plants put out far more uranium and thorium emissions than nuclear plants are permitted to emit. Well, that's government, so it has to be right.

18,000 people died during Japan's Fukushima meltdown. Every one of those deaths was due to the earthquake and tsunami, not a single one to radiation exposure.

America is one of the few nations that is cutting its CO2 emissions. Fracking has turned natural gas into a feasible source of electricity, replacing coal, which emits twice as much CO2 per unit of energy.

Recovery from the 2020 economic depression may not be too swift. Economic growth is slowed when the national debt is high, which it most certainly is. Also, too many Americans are receiving more money from the government for not working than they would earn if they returned to work.

---

85. WSJ, Holman W. Jenkins, Jr., *Climate Crowd ignores a Scientific Fraud*, 4/15/16

Since 1980, the federal government has spent $500 billion (in 2017 dollars) on education and an additional $250 billion on Head Start for low-income preschoolers. Studies have found that students in older grades who experienced Head Start have been no more advanced than those who did not. In other words, Head Start wasn't worth the money. The results would have been better and less expensive if education were handled completely by the private sector. With government out of the picture, prosperous people would help pay to meet the needs of others.

In striving for bigger government, the media is setting up its possible demise. Big government eventually attracts leaders whose desire to exercise power is pathological. They want all the power, with worshipful followers and control of the news. People in media would be among the first to be arrested.

CONSTITUTIONALIST JUDGES

The judges placed on U.S. courts by the Trump administration are "constitutionalists," meaning they interpret the ordinary meaning of legal texts. They let laws stand even if they personally disagree with them.

Some judges appointed by previous presidents believe in a "living Constitution," meaning they rule on what they think a law ought to say rather than on what it actually says. If they consider a law to be wrong, they overrule it.

Confusion results when both judges and legislatures make laws. Also, most judges who override legislative law favor larger and more intrusive government. Wrong direction; we need smaller government, not larger.

A prominent example of the living Constitution approach is the 1973 Roe v. Wade decision. By a vote of 7-to-2, Supreme Court judges struck down abortion laws at all levels of the government. A net of five individuals overruling many duly-elected legislatures was elitist and highly undemocratic.

I personally approve of abortions, but Roe v. Wade should be reversed. Let each state determine the exact legal conditions for taking the life of a fetus. It's okay if the state laws differ. That's called diversity.

Judges should be subject to term limits of, say, eighteen years, not for life. To steal a phrase, this would help make the courts "living institutions."

Judges need not be lawyers. Common sense may suffice.

HOW MOST OF OUR MONEY IS CREATED

Well over 90% of our money supply consists of bank deposits. Here's where those numbers come from:

Let's say the Federal Reserve Bank, bidding higher than anyone else for Treasury securities, induces me to sell $10,000 of my Treasury securities. Through intermediaries, the Fed writes $10,000 in my bank account. That's new money.

Let's say that you, dear reader, happen to have an account at my bank, although we don't know each other. You request a loan from the bank, and the bank credits your account with, say, $7,000. That's also new money, made possible by the increase in the bank's reserves from the Fed's previous $10,000 deposit.

You then pay out a check for $7,000 to someone who has performed a service for you. He deposits it in his bank.

His bank can then lend, say, $5,000 to a fourth person. The banking system then has $22,000 of new money.

On it goes, with each bank usually lending over half of its new reserves. When the final penny is lent, the nation will probably hold more than $30,000 of new money, including the Fed's original $10,000 payment plus additional funds the banks created themselves.

The capacity of banks to create money is called the "Multiplier Effect." It's legal, and it's a good thing.

The Fed's new money is a different story. The Fed has created far too much of it, causing the buying power of the dollar to deteriorate markedly. It's not the fault of the banks. The actions of the Federal Reserve Bank are wrong all too often.

Turn the Petroleum Reserve into an Oil Bank[86]

The Strategic Petroleum Reserve (SPR) holds 645 million barrels of crude oil, which is 60.7% of USA oil inventories. It could supply U.S. crude needs for almost a month all by itself.

The SPR has cost the government $19.2 billion to fill, not including the heavy cost of hollowing out five huge salt domes in Texas and Louisiana. The government has lost money on the deal. What else is new?

In 45 years, the SPR has been used only three times for emergency purposes. On each occasion, if the SPR had not existed, sufficient oil would have been found to meet the need, probably at a higher but not insufferable price.

The SPR should be closed. Since this is not politically palatable, Professor Steve Hanke of Johns Hopkins University suggests turning the SPR into an oil bank. (This column cites his figures, which change every day.)

The government would sell a series of out-of-the-money call options on its oil. For example, in August, with the price of oil at $30, the SPR might sell an option that gives the buyer of the option, or any subsequent owner, the right to buy a specified quantity of oil from the SPR by the third Friday in December at a price of $35 a barrel. If the price rises to or above $35 before that date, the owner of the option could, at any time in the interim, "call" the option, take delivery of the specified amount of oil, and pay $35 a barrel. If the price does not reach $35 by the third Friday

---

86. Forbes, Steve Hanke, *Trump: Transform the U.S. Strategic Petroleum Reserve into an Oil Bank,* 9/27/19.

in December, or if the option owner fails to call the option, the option expires, and no crude is released.

Did you get all that? It's okay if you didn't.

These conditional sales would generate revenue, lessen price fluctuations, and eventually liquefy SPR's huge supply. Best of all, it would usually be the market, not a government official, that determines when to release the oil.

FLAT INCOME TAXES

Individuals should be subject to a very low tax rate on income, with no exemptions or deductions. Tax returns could be filled out on postcards. Millions of dollars spent on preparing tax returns could be saved. (The lawyers and accountants who assist people with their returns would have choice words to say about this. So would some of the 94,000 IRS employees no longer needed.)

Corporations should not be taxed at all. They're just associations of people, and people are taxed individually.

Long-term capital gains are the most foolish tax of all. Every time the rates on long-term gains have been lowered, revenues have come pouring into the IRS, as people take profits on stocks they've owned for a while.

THE U.S. NEEDS A SPACE FORCE [87]

The United States needs a Space Force.

Congress and the Defense Department are resisting, believing that assets in space should be run by the Air Force to support wars on the earth's surface.

China has other ideas. According to Lieutenant General Steven Kwast

87. Imprimis, Lt. General Steven L. Kwast, *The Urgent Need for a United States Space Force*, January 2020.

(Ret.), writing in *Imprimis*, a Hillsdale College publication, China is striving to achieve space technology that can shut down our computer systems, disable our power grid, and paralyze our military.

America should do the following:

- Declare by Act of Congress that the space from the earth to the moon is the responsibility of the United States.

- Utilizing China's practices, the Space Force should maximize the contributions of the private sector to protect America and the space industry.

- It should capture energy from solar power in space and deliver unlimited amounts to every human on the planet without power plants or power lines. (Those who produce oil, coal, and natural gas will have a little something to say about this.)

- Build a low-cost, secure internet that enables everyone to connect safely.

- Obtain abundant natural resources from the moon.

- Revolutionize manufacturing, develop life-saving medicines, and establish cities in space.

- Defend earth against small asteroids.

- Manage the eyes of hurricanes and tornadoes with energy from space.

Technologies exist to achieve these goals. The developments would cut costs here on earth.

The following unsettling quote provides ample justification for the ideas expressed by Lt. General Kwast above. It comes from an article in the June 2, 2020 issue of the Washington Examiner. The quote is drawn from a recent book called *The Kill Chain, Defending America in the Future of High-Tech Warfare,* by Christian Brose, a former staff director of the Senate Armed Services Committee:

"Over the past decade, in U.S. war games against China, the United States has a nearly perfect record: We have lost almost every single time."

Jamie McIntyre, author of the Washington Examiner article, adds, "Most members of Congress do not know this – even though they should. But in the Department of Defense, (the sorry record of the U.S. war games) is a well-known fact."

SMALLER GOVERNMENT DESPERATELY NEEDED

July 27, 2020: Observing the violence in the streets, Sarah believes the quality of American life has deteriorated.

It certainly has, Sarah. In fact, the liberal media is not revealing the full extent of the current destruction.

Here's the basic reason for the public violence: For more than a century, since the administration of Theodore Roosevelt, the government sector of the United States has grown from 10% of the GDP to something like 37%. Ever more laws and regulations have been enacted.

Laws and regulations apply force, which is a form of violence. Government violence begets the public violence we're now seeing in American cities, especially in Washington and Oregon, whose state governments have been especially large and intrusive for decades.

Joe Biden intends to apply force all the more, making government even bigger and more intrusive. This would be disastrous. Most uses of governmental force make things worse, especially for the poor.

Unlike most presidents, President Trump is unafraid of the overwhelmingly liberal press. One hopes he will use this attribute to begin the long process of cutting back government. The government now is about as large as it was four years ago.

Mr. Trump may not feel comfortable about doing this. Reducing the platform on which he stands doesn't seem to fit his character. But he has touted "drain the swamp," a slogan that means cutting back government, does it not? It's time for him to consider the bureaucracy an enemy and begin this job in earnest. It is desperately needed.

WISDOM OF THOMAS SOWELL

In my opinion, wisdom is a combination of intelligence, common sense, and facility of expression. Thomas Sowell, black economist and newspaper columnist, possesses these qualities in abundance. Here are some of his pithy sayings about public affairs:

- Black families survived centuries of slavery and generations of Jim Crow, but disintegrated because of the expansion of the welfare state.

- Decisions should not be put in the hands of people who pay no price for being wrong.

- The big word on the left is compassion. But their big agenda is dependency.

- A pervasive political vision of our time is the vision of liberals as compassionate and conservatives as less caring.

- Ideas that don't work are concentrated in institutions where ideas don't have to work to survive.

- Today's problems are a result of yesterday's solutions.

- The real minimum wage is zero. This is what inexperienced and low-skilled people receive because of legislation making it illegal for employers to pay them what they're worth.

- Compassion is a willingness to spend taxpayer money in ways that will increase the spender's chances of getting reelected.

- Many countries started out redistributing wealth and ended up redistributing poverty.

CHAPTER 11 – BENIGN POLICIES

GOVERNMENT'S ESSENTIAL AND BENIGN DUTIES

MOST USES OF GOVERNMENT FORCE are counterintuitive. The actual long-term results are opposite to the intended results. But the following duties of government are not counterintuitive. They're essential and benign. The lives of all Americans would be much improved if U.S. governments at every level fulfilled these duties and nothing more:

- Foster individual liberty

- Protect private property

- Enforce contracts

- Adjudicate lawsuits

- Prevent people from directly hurting others by force or fraud (the police power)

- Enact and enforce election laws

- Enact and enforce immigration laws

- Defend the nation.

These eight duties, especially the first two, are bulwarks of a successful society. Without them, misery results.

American governments have performed these duties reasonably well. There are many exceptions, of course. Government-supported unions, for example, have kept bad cops from being fired. But for the most part, America has done pretty well with these duties – a key reason why the nation has prospered.

But since about 1900, U.S. federal, state, and local governments have enacted increasing numbers of laws and regulations whose long-term effects are damaging. When the sections, subsections, and sub-subsections of the laws and regulations are counted, I'm guessing that government's harmful uses of force number at least in the hundreds of thousands and possibly the millions.

After a law or regulation is enacted, problems eventually result. A governmental solution is then devised as a solution, but this eventually makes the problem worse. More government solutions follow to correct the problems, but these create yet more problems. It's a downward cycle.

Thomas Sowell: "Today's problems are a result of yesterday's solutions."

The use of government force is still advancing. The protection of individual liberty and private property has partly been shunted aside. If government keeps growing, America will descend into misery.

In his book, "Private Governance: Creating Order in Economic and Social Life," Edward Peter Stringham makes a good case that at least some of the eight benign duties presented above should be handled by the private sector. This might apply to enforcing contracts and adjudicating lawsuits. To some extent, it might also apply to the police power.

PROTECTING USERS OF FACILITIES

A reader wrote, "If America becomes a libertarian nation and most of the nation's public facilities are owned privately, how are the users of those facilities protected?"

The users would eventually learn to take responsibility for protecting themselves. Government fosters too much concern about safety. Mr. Obama's political ads citing a woman the government looked out for from cradle to grave was outrageous. He wanted the government to be mom and dad, with the rest of us children. Guess who'd be the Number One Dad?

If a place is truly unsafe and someone gets hurt, the owner gets sued. The lawsuit encourages other owners to shape up.

In a libertarian society, the judiciary becomes the most important branch of government.

FREEDOM

As long as they're not directly hurting others, people should live as they please. They should be allowed to live with or marry whomever they like, whatever the gender. Women should be allowed to abort their fetuses. People should be allowed to hurt themselves with alcohol, drugs, the sale of body parts, or suicide. All these matters are none of the government's business. Attempts to improve life by force only make things worse.

A QUICK STAB AT DEVELOPING A TAX SYSTEM

June 4, 2020. Eventually, all government revenues would be voluntary gifts from citizens. This would produce plenty of money.

But in the meantime, here are preliminary ideas for government revenues. To minimize words, I use the present tense:

Government's basic costs are national defense, the police, the court systems, and the costs of leadership. No State Department. No embassies. No government foreign aid. No UN membership. A much smaller government has nothing to do with education, imposes no regulations, pays no welfare of any kind, and no longer has anything to do with the monetary system or the economy. Government charges no corporate taxes and no property taxes. Courts charge no fees.

Personal income is the sole source of revenues. Taxable income includes earned income, dividends, long-term and short-term gains, and property insurance proceeds less premiums paid.

The rate is 7%, applying from the first to the last dollar, with no deductions nor exemptions.

- The feds take 4% to cover defense and immigration costs.
- Local governments, which have most of the police, take 2%.
- The states take 1%.

(These governmental bodies, separate entities all, would not permit themselves to be dumped into one bucket. The nerve!)

INDUCING THE RICH TO HELP THE POOR

June 17, 2019. Most people believe that private citizens are not altruistic enough to take care of the needy. Government has to do it. Many television shows have portrayed wealthy businessmen as bad guys.

Most are not. The preeminent bad guys are government and its nefarious partners, unions.

When government raises tax revenue by force, as it does now, and pays it out to some groups but not to others, this arouses envy and resentment. The natural response is to try to beat the system, with everyone out for themselves. Big government promotes selfishness.

If government were much reduced, people would take responsibility for their own actions. Self-guided people tend to be altruistic. Numerous private organizations and corporations would raise money from the prosperous and pay it to the needy. In New York City in the 1890s, there were dozens of such agencies. Oh yes, there were poor people in New York in the 1890s, even cholera. But most of the poor were recent immigrants. Morale was generally high, and people quickly rose up out of the gutter.

With tax rates low and government pulling way back, you can bet that prosperous people of today would provide helping hands and financial assistance.

The media would assist, promulgating messages such as, "Mr. Big Bucks of this community has displayed his wealth with a huge home and stupendous yacht. But in the past few years, he has given little to alleviate poverty." This would probably enliven the gentleman's charitable impulses.

Many government policies unintentionally hurt the poor. If these policies were reversed, the poor would need less help from others.

If government stopped all welfare, would private parties actually step forward to help?

Of course they would. With government backing way off and taxes much lower, most people would genuinely feel that the needs of society would be part of their personal responsibility. It would be a giving society. The underclass would flourish.

THE BEST LIBERTARIAN GOVERNMENT[88]

What's the best libertarian government the modern world has known?

His name was Sir John James Cowperthwaite, a British civil servant and financial secretary of Hong Kong from 1961 to 1971.

Hong Kong was one of the poorest places on earth when Cowperthwaite arrived in 1945. He was asked to find ways in which the government could boost the post-war economy. Having observed that the economy was already recovering swiftly with no government intervention, he demurred.

---

88. Wikipedia, *John James Cowperthwaite*

He promoted free trade, low taxation, limited state intervention in the economy, a distrust of industrial planning, and sound money. Hong Kong imposed no tariffs on products it imported, even when the opposing countries imposed tariffs on Hong Kong products they imported.

Cowperthwaite turned down subordinates who wanted to collect GDP and other statistics. Gathering statistics, he felt, would uncover problems the bureaucrats would want to solve. If a problem needed a solution, it was better to rely on the people, with free markets, to do the job. When asked for the key thing poor countries should do to improve their growth, he replied, "Abolish the office of national statistics."

His policies helped Hong Kong become the freest economy in the world. It also had the fastest growing economy in the world.

Did it become a den of inequity? Of course not. It is government that generates inequity. Free markets reduce it.

What's the first thing the U.S. government should do to emulate Hong Kong?

Stop collecting statistics.

DECISIVENESS

After a liberal friend and I had a pleasant disagreement about public affairs, I wrote him the following:

You seem to enjoy having pleasant discussions about public affairs, but not making decisions about them. I enjoy such controversy, especially if it enables me to learn. I also enjoy being decisive about public affairs.

If I were a liberal, I'd be indecisive too. Let's say I were trying to choose between two government policies. After taking into account the hidden, long-term consequences, I couldn't decide which one I'd choose, because they'd both be unfavorable.

Except for the eight essential and benign policies presented in this chapter, a libertarian, like Sir Cowperthwaite, is prone to say, "Let the people work it out."

Assume the people try, but are unable to solve the problem because too few people came forward to help. They might return to me as president and ask me to do the job.

I would respond, "Keep at it. I've cut tax rates to make more funds available". If things get worse, more people would then come forward. Once they do, and they learn how to get the job done, they will end up resolving the matter better and less expensively than government could possibly achieve.

I fervently hope there will come a day, before America fails completely, when the bulk of voters realize that solutions to social and economic problems can never be perfect, but that private solutions, in the long run, generally make things better, while almost all government solutions make things worse.

To Help the Poor, Embrace Human Nature

April 9, 2018. A caring friend wrote, "After seeing so many people sleeping on San Francisco sidewalks, I feel complicit in the crime of indifference. We cannot blindly trust human nature. Government must prevent corporate profits from running the nation."

Profits did not cause San Francisco's homelessness. Quite the opposite, profits were *suppressed* by the laws and regulations that reduced home building. With San Francisco's economy growing but homes increasingly less available, the prices of homes rose so much that not even the middle class could afford them, never mind the poor.

The states with the largest and most intrusive governments – California, New York, and Hawaii – have the highest number of homeless per 100,000 people.[89] Big-government liberalism doesn't solve social

---

89. I obtained this information from the Web.

and economic problems. It causes them.

Government efforts to control the economy hurt the poor more than they help. If government just let the economy take care of itself, the poor would gain wealth faster than the rich, and the gap between the two would narrow. The gap would never close, of course, because capabilities vary from one person to another.

You advocate the suppression of human nature. This would help no one except bureaucrats, who squash human nature big time with government controls.

We should instead embrace human nature, including the desire to make money. Profit opportunities abound in helping people meet their needs.

With tax rates low and government backing way off, private organizations would raise billions of dollars from the rich and pay it to the needy. The competition between the organizations would keep their profits small in comparison with government's massive costs.

THE BEST WAY TO HELP THE POOR

Most conservatives maintain that a growing economy is a good way to help the poor. They're right; it's a good way. But it's not the best way.

The best way is to get government off their backs. The poor are down because government, without meaning to, keeps them down. With government slimmed way down, the poor would pull themselves up nicely.

STEALING

A fellow comes to your door, points a gun at you, and demands money for him to cover his expenses. This is certainly stealing.

The second time, he points a gun and demands money. He'll keep a little of it and pay the bulk to a needy neighbor. This is stealing.

The third time, he points a gun and says the neighborhood has appointed him their agent to demand your money. He will keep a little of it and pay the bulk to a needy neighbor. This is stealing, too.

The fourth time, the government comes to your door, points a gun, and demands your money. More than half will pay for the government's enormous bureaucracy, the crony capitalists, and interest on the debt. Considerably less than half will go to the needy. This is called taxation.

PURPOSES

October 26, 2020. A friend wrote that whichever candidate wins the election, some groups are going to be sorely disappointed, to say the least.

My response: It is not the purpose of elective politics to avoid disappointment. It is the purpose of elective politics to avoid civil war.

THE BEST WAY TO GET GOVERNMENT OFF PEOPLE'S BACKS

Don't make deductible gifts to charities. Pay the taxes and give *after-tax* money to people who are deeply engaged in the political process, striving to remove Democrats and liberal Republicans from the U.S. Congress. Liberals are the ones who keep the poor down. They don't intend to, but the long-term consequences of their laws and regulations have this effect.

My favorite organization for removing liberals from Congress is the Club for Growth, of Washington, DC, which engages in the nitty gritty of political campaigns. Numerous conservative members of Congress would not have gained that position without the support of the Club for Growth.

PANDEMIC IN A LIBERTARIAN SOCIETY

If a libertarian society is attacked by a pandemic, the government would do nothing about it. A great deal of advice would be given in the media and on the Internet, some good, some bad, but none by government. With no fear of antitrust lawsuits, companies and associations would plan how to meet the crisis. Every citizen would deal with the matter as they chose. Widespread immunity would be achieved as quickly as possible.

A LIBERTARIAN NATION

Under a libertarian government, the country would become a giving society. People would fulfill their own needs, yes, but most people, especially the prosperous, would be concerned about the health and happiness of the entire society. Even now, 100 million Americans make charitable gifts each year, with the average household donating around $3,000 a year.[90] These amounts would increase exponentially.

Violence begets violence. Government is the only part of society authorized to use force, as I've stated many times in this book. As government has become monstrous, force has permeated society, causing violence and riots such as we've seen lately.

With government pulling way back, the use of force would be far less prevalent, and incidence of violence would become less common.

Sharply limiting U.S. governments would raise morale, increase self-reliance and caring, and improve the quality of life across the land, especially for the poor.

Society's needs, other than those satisfied by government's proper duties, above, should be fulfilled by private parties operating for profit or by associations of those who care. Competition among them minimizes

90. WSJ, Karl Zinsmeister, *The War on Philanthropy*. 1/9/20.

costs. The more needs that arise, the more people would come forward to meet them.

Private giving would increase exponentially. Even with a nation as large as ours, it would be a giving society. People would genuinely feel, "We're all in this together."